CHARTISM

THE VICTORIAN LIBRARY

CHARTISM

A NEW ORGANIZATION OF THE PEOPLE

WILLIAM LOVETT

AND

JOHN COLLINS

WITH AN INTRODUCTION BY

ASA BRIGGS

LEICESTER UNIVERSITY PRESS

NEW YORK: HUMANITIES PRESS

1969

First published in 1840
Victorian Library edition published in 1969 by
Leicester University Press

Distributed in North America by
Humanities Press Inc., New York

Introduction copyright © Asa Briggs 1969

Printed in Great Britain by
Unwin Brothers Limited, Old Woking, Surrey
Introduction set in Monotype Modern Extended 7

SBN 7185 5006 4

THE VICTORIAN LIBRARY

There is a growing demand for the classics of Victorian literature in many fields, in history, in literature, in sociology and economics, in the natural sciences. Hitherto this demand has been met, in the main, from the second-hand market. But the prices of second-hand books are rising sharply, and the supply of them is very uncertain. It is the object of this series, THE VICTORIAN LIBRARY, to make some of these classics available again, at a reasonable cost. Since most of the volumes in it are reprinted photographically from the first edition, or another chosen because it has some special value, an accurate text is ensured. Each work carries a substantial introduction, by a well-known authority on the author or his subject, and a bibliographical note on the text.

The volumes necessarily vary in size. In planning the newly-set pages the designer, Arthur Lockwood, has maintained a consistent style for the principal features. The uniform design of binding and jackets provides for ready recognition of the various books in the series when shelved under different subject classifications.

Recommendation of titles for THE VICTORIAN LIBRARY and of scholars to contribute the Introductions is made by a joint committee of the Board of the University Press and the Victorian Studies Centre of the University of Leicester.

INTRODUCTION

William Lovett, a self-taught craftsman, was in his fortieth year when he wrote *Chartism; A New Organization of the People*. It was published in 1840 under the imprint of three radical publishers—Henry Hetherington, John Cleave and James Watson—who were close friends and associates in what Lovett called as part of the title of his well-known autobiography "struggles . . . in pursuit of Bread, Knowledge and Freedom".

The sense of struggle was as basic to this group of men—and there were others like them scattered throughout the country—as was the common culture shaped by self-education which they all shared and the common ideal to which they all aspired—co-operative association for "the illumination and salvation of our race". Their organ, the *Poor Man's Guardian*, founded by Hetherington in December 1830, stated boldly that it was "established contrary to Law, to try the power of 'Might' against 'Right' ". In place of the official Government red stamp it defiantly displayed a black stamp bearing the words "Knowledge is Power".

The *Poor Man's Guardian* ceased publication in December 1835. During its existence it had encouraged working men to seek political power for themselves to realize co-operative principles. It thereby provided a link between the working-men's Owenism of the 1820s and the Chartism of the 1830s. It familiarized its sponsors with imprisonment. Watson, who had learnt his radicalism in Leeds, was imprisoned in 1833 for selling the unstamped *Guardian*, one of three spells of imprisonment: Hetherington also was imprisoned three times, and Cleave twice. The free press agitation succeeded, in

Lovett's words, written later in his career, in creating "a public opinion sufficiently powerful to cause the Government to give up the *fourpenny stamp* upon newspapers and to substitute a *penny stamp* instead" in 1836. At the same time—and this was Lovett's view nearer in time to the event—there could be no hope of really free and open political argument until the stamp duty was totally repealed, which it eventually was, after middle-class pressure, in 1855.

The relationship between working-class pressure and middle-class pressure to secure political and social reforms was the chief, though not the only, question which concerned all radical politicians between the late 1820s and the early 1850s. Discussion of it was sharp and often urgent for two main reasons. First, many of the key decisions which had to be taken about practical, political tactics pivoted on attitudes towards class relations. Second, both working-class and middle-class political organizations recognized that they could not take for granted militant class consciousness on the part of their own groups. In 1835, on the eve of the change in the stamp rate, Lovett realized that through the free press agitation he and his friends had "collected together", in his own words, "a goodly number of active and influential workingmen". In fact, the process of collecting them together had gone back earlier in time. The British Association for Promoting Co-operative Knowledge (1829), of which Lovett was secretary, had been succeeded by the National Union of the Working Classes and Others (1831), a universal suffrage organization which provided a second, this time an organizational, link between working-men's Owenism in the late 1820s and Chartism in the 1830s. It was in 1831 that Hetherington in his *Penny Papers for the People*, the predecessor of the *Poor Man's Guardian*, wrote that "the middling classes will never wish the poor and the despised 'mob', as even *they* call the *working classes*, to have equal power with themselves".

There had been debate inside the small National Union as to whether the phrase "and others" should be added to the name of the association. Not surprisingly, therefore, when the free press agitation reached its climax in 1835 and further forms of political struggle were being considered, the question naturally arose, as Lovett put it, as to "whether we could form or maintain a union found exclusively of this class [the working class] and of such men [the supporters of the free press agitation]". Lovett felt that they could. Desire both for "union" and for "independence" had to be fostered. "We were the more induced to try the experiment as the working classes had not hitherto evinced that discrimination and independent spirit in the management of their political affairs which we are desirous to see."

It was in this spirit of mutual self-help that the London Working Men's Association was founded in June 1836. Its first objective was "to draw into one bond of *unity* the *intelligent* and *influential* portion of the working classes in town and country" and its eighth and last was "to form a library of reference and useful information; to maintain a place where they can associate for mental improvement, and where their brethren from the country can meet with kindred minds activated by one great motive—that of benefiting politically, socially, and morally, the useful classes". Class relationships were dealt with frankly but cautiously in this first L W M A manifesto. "All classes in society" were to be granted "equal political and social rights", yet "the interests of the working classes", in particular, were to be specially studied within "society in general". "Though the persons forming this Association will be at all times disposed to cooperate with all those who seek to promote the happiness of the multitude, yet being convinced from experience that the division of interests in the various classes, in the present state of things, is too often destructive of that union of sentiment which is essential to the prosecution of any great object, they have resolved to confine their members as far as practicable to the working classes."

Even then the question of the complications of class relationships did not end. The boundaries of the "useful classes" were not easy to define, particularly in London, where there was little large-scale industry and where there had been long-standing and close, if sometimes confused, association between small employers and working men in many forms of political activity, from struggles to control vestries to efforts to secure legislation. "Well wishers" might limit the effectiveness of independent action by the LWMA, but what of friendly shopkeepers and booksellers, even of professional men? Trade unionism had made working men conscious of the special interests of "wealth producers", but even in relation to trade unionism, Owen's own ambivalence in thinking and talking about "class" had not been without its influence. The LWMA, a small body, personal and self-reliant, was forced to leave class questions relatively open. "As there are great differences of opinion as to where the line should be drawn which separates the working classes from the other portions of society, they leave to the members themselves to determine whether the candidate to be proposed is eligible to become a member."

Since Lovett was the author of most of the LWMA manifestoes and addresses and he deliberately used them as basic documentary material in the writing of his autobiography, it is necessary to note carefully both the tone of the argument and the qualifications that were introduced into it. He was anxious to create what he called "a moral, reflecting, yet energetic public opinion", yet he eschewed "violence or commotion". He wanted the LWMA to be selective: "judicious selection" should keep out "the drunken and the immoral". "Private conduct" had to be impeccable to match public principle. Numbers were less important than quality. Almost every manifesto or address severely criticized "the drunken revelry of the pot-house" or "the fumes of the tap room". The moral aspect of reform was always emphasized. "Could corruption sit in the judgement seat—empty-headed importance in the senate house—money-getting hypocrisy in the pulpit—and debauchery, fanaticism, poverty, and crime stalk triumphantly through the land —if the millions were educated in a knowledge of their rights?" It follows from passages of this kind that Lovett was interested, above all else, in turning the working classes, as he saw them, into "a band of brothers . . . setting an example of propriety to their neighbours". To him this was not the rhetoric of reform, but its *sine qua non*.

Yet he was aware of what he called "the present state of things". While much of the language of the manifestoes and addresses recalls, like the Charter, the language of eighteenth-century radicalism—"happiness", "improvement", "universal good"—we are in a very different world from that of Wilkes or for that matter of Paine. Lovett, a craftsman, who had made his way to London from Cornwall in 1821, knew that industrialization had changed the scene—that "the present state of things" was different from what it had been fifty years earlier. "Is the *Manufacturer* and *Capitalist*", a later LWMA address demanded, "whose exclusive monopoly of the combined powers of wood, iron and steam enables them to cause the destitution of thousands, and who have an interest in forcing labour down to the *minimum* reward, fit to represent the interests of working men? Is the *Master*, whose interest it is to purchase labour at the cheapest rate, a fit representative for the *Workman*, whose interest it is to get the most he can for his labour?" Six years earlier, O'Brien, in the *Poor Man's Guardian* (30 July 1831) had warned its readers that they had nothing to expect from "little property men", "petty masters" or "middle men", and Lovett in a speech at the Rotunda in September 1831 had warned working men not to be "captivated with a promise, pleased with a bauble and tickled with a straw" (*ibid.*, 1 October 1831).

Middle-class radicals might be employed by Lovett in the campaign for the Six Points of the Charter, which opened with a public meeting at the Crown and Anchor Tavern in the Strand in February 1837, and colonial issues might figure more than industrial issues in the first petition which was sent to Parliament after the opening of the campaign. Yet as soon as the LWMA began to

send "missionaries" into the provinces—the most important of all its activities—it was brought into touch with
the brute facts of working-class conditions. It was not
Lovett but H. S. Tremenheere, the sociologically-minded
government inspector, who wrote that "great employers
who collected large bodies of labourers on wild districts"
were unwilling at that time "to acknowledge . . . the
dependence of moral and intellectual conditions on its
material surroundings". Five years, indeed, before the
LWMA missionaries moved out into the provinces, the
Poor Man's Guardian (17 November 1832) had described
vividly—and with relevant statistics—the plight of
weavers in Huddersfield, nailers in Halesowen, strawplait
workers in Dunstable and lace-makers in Nottingham.
Between 1832 and 1837 the situation had been exacerbated
by three additional circumstances—the failure of organized large-scale trade unionism; the new Poor Law of
1834, described by Hetherington as "a murderer's death
blow to the operative classes"; and the beginning of
economic depression following the financial crisis of 1836.
The fact that radicals like O'Connell were hostile to trade
unionism, that many of them supported the new Poor
Law of 1834 on Benthamite grounds, and that unemploy-
ment was an experience they usually did not know
directly, accentuated tendencies making for specifically
working-class protest.

The forms of protest and the styles of agitation were
often uncongenial to Lovett and his friends, although
they were of the very essence of Chartism as we understand
it and as contemporaries like Carlyle and Disraeli
understood it. Chartism was in a very real sense what
Carlyle called it, "the cry of pent-up millions suffering
under a diseased condition of society". Its basic strength
lay in its power to unify discontented men in all parts of
the country. The Charter, published in London in May
1838, provided a rallying point. "In less than twelve
months from the date of its publication", Lovett wrote,
"upwards of a million people had declared in its favour,
and it was going on rapidly enlisting new converts and
earnest supporters." Many of them, he went on, became

convinced of "the justice, the practicability and the efficiency" of the Chartist answer.

There was no more enthusiastic Chartist than Lovett. Nonetheless, he watched the rise of Feargus O'Connor as Chartist leader with unconcealed distaste and alarm. The origins of their animosity were both temperamental and political: they went back in time, moreover, deep into the London radical politics of the earlier 1830s before the Charter was drafted. It was before, not after, the Charter was drafted that O'Connor condemned the L W M A and Lovett attacked O'Connor for his "self idolatry". "Sir, you might have beaten the big drum of your own vanity", Lovett exclaimed in what is perhaps the most quoted passage from all his writings, "till you grew sick of its music, and revelled in your own vanity till common sense taught your audience that the sacrifice was greater than the benefit, had you been pleased to excuse us from worshipping at your altar. But no, your own vain self must be supreme—you must be the 'leader of the people' —and from the first moment that we resolved to form an association of workingmen and called upon them to manage their own affairs, and *dispense with leadership of any description*; we have had *you* and *patriots of your feelings continually in arms against us.*"

The Charter was a rallying point, but there was never unanimity amongst the Chartists. There was clearly an immense distance between Lovett and O'Connor. There were also local and regional differences which need to be explained in something more than psychological or political terms. Leaving aside the provinces, where Chartism spread fast and where O'Connor quickly gained a position of national ascendancy, London itself was divided. The L W M A was one force in the fragmented radical politics of London, but not the only one, not even the most important one. On its right were bodies seeking closer regular association with middle-class radicals: on its left were bodies like the East London Democratic Association (1837), the West London Democratic Federation (1838), the Central National Association (1837) and the London Democratic Association (1838), with numerous splinter groups. In the background were radical clubs and associations, some with older pedigrees, and trade societies, each with its own distinctive composition and leadership. There was ample scope, therefore, both for the presentation of radical arguments and for the fomenting of radical antagonisms.

The General Convention of the Industrious Classes, which met in London in February 1839, moved to Birmingham in May and returned as a rump in July, was the main theatre of Chartist debate. It was there, in what was thought of as a "People's Parliament", that all the differences about tactics and about class relationships came out into the open. In welcoming the delegates to Birmingham, one Chartist emphasized how important it was that they should work out their own salvation . . . "no matter what the middle classes might say". The debate continued in the "localities", as the Chartists called them, and went on after the Convention had dispersed, Parliament had rejected the Charter, and many Chartists were imprisoned. It was a debate which touched on almost every issue which has arisen in mass politics ever since, from the scope and purposes of constitutional change to the use of force. Unity was impossible to achieve, not least in the metropolis, where the General Metropolitan Charter Association and the London Association of United Chartists had both failed by the spring of 1840 to unite London Chartists. "Before the end of the year", more than one Chartist had exclaimed in March 1839, "we shall have universal suffrage or death"— "death or glory", O'Connor added with a flourish. Yet by July the rump of the Convention agreed by twelve votes to six that "although it is the duty of the Convention to participate in all the people's dangers, it is no part of our duty to create danger unnecessarily, either for ourselves or others. To create it for ourselves would be folly: to create it for others would be a crime."

Recent writing on Chartism has tended to deal briefly with the history of the Convention, yet the Convention repays close attention both in its own and in a bigger context. The final decision to dissolve it, taken on the chairman's casting vote, saw Chartists of quite different persuasions voting side by side, as did Harney, the revolutionary Chartist, and Hetherington, the old pioneer. Lovett, who served as secretary of the Convention, had been arrested in Birmingham on 5 July and taken to Warwick gaol: in August he was sentenced, along with John Collins, a local Chartist, to twelve months' imprisonment. Harney, however, who had also been arrested, was released. The contrast between their treatment raises interesting questions. Certainly, while Harney had hoped for revolution in 1839, as he did later, Lovett never lost his faith in legality. He had insisted upon consulting a barrister to ascertain the legality of the rules of the Convention before it met, and it was his protest against the actions of the Metropolitan Police in suppressing disorders in the Birmingham Bull Ring—"a wanton, flagrant and unjust outrage . . . made upon the people of Birmingham by a bloodthirsty and unconstitutional force from London"—which led to his arrest. When he was ill-treated in Warwick Gaol it was to the radical M.P. for Westminster, J. T. Leader, and to Lord Brougham that he complained. He had never believed in a revolution by force, yet at his trial the Attorney General had ordered that a display of weapons of various kinds said to have been collected in the Bull Ring should be displayed to connect Lovett with "the riots and burnings that had taken place there". Not surprisingly, Lovett was to write in a later judgement, which perhaps did not go very deep, that the cause of the Chartist difficulties in 1839 was the revolutionary talk which had alienated other sections of the community. "We were fast gathering up the favourable opinion of the Middle, as well as of the Working Classes, when the violent ravings about physical force, by O'Connor, Stephens and Oastler scared them from our ventures: they, doubtlessly conceiving that they had better put up with known evils, than trust to an unknown remedy, proposed to be effected by such desperate means."

It was while he was imprisoned in Warwick Gaol that Lovett wrote *Chartism; A New Organization of the People*.

It appeared under his name with the word "cabinet-maker" added and the name of John Collins who was described as a "tool-maker". The writing of the book relieved the tedium and monotony of prison life, and the final copy of the manuscript was smuggled out. It said nothing that had not been said before by Lovett equally forcefully and in much the same language, but the fact that he had been imprisoned on unfair grounds gave it special significance and the fact that many other Chartists of very different persuasions were imprisoned during the summer and autumn of 1839 gave it immediate point. Its stress on the need for education and for organization was certainly not new, but the argument now had something of the force of an object lesson. "If, therefore, we should succeed in arousing the attention of the millions to the great importance of the subjects treated of in this pamphlet," Lovett ended the preface, "we think we shall not have suffered twelve months' imprisonment in vain."

The book was divided into three main parts—a somewhat rambling introduction stating the Chartist case; a set of specific rules and regulations for a new association to be called the National Association of the United Kingdom for Promoting the Political and Social Improvement of the People, followed by a general section on "the benefits of organization"; and an essay on education. In each section there are echoes of earlier writing. Thus, the words of hope in the very first paragraph—"the spark once struck is inextinguishable, and will go on extending and radiating with increasing power"—recall the last objective in the original manifesto of the National Union of the Working Classes—"to concentrate into one focus a knowledge of moral and political economy, that all classes of society may be enlightened by its radiation". The set of rules in the second part follows in several places the set of rules of the LWMA. The essay on education is written along the same lines as an Address to the Working Classes on the subject of education prepared by the LWMA in 1837 and later printed in Lovett's autobiography.

There were differences, however, and it is instructive to compare in detail the proposed rules for the National Association with those of the LWMA. The former are more diffuse on social questions than the latter and more specific on points of educational detail. There is no reference to the working classes at all, and the first object of the National Association is said to be "to unite, in one general body, persons of all creeds, classes, and opinions, who are desirous to promote the political and social improvement of the people." The second clause refers to "the industrious classes" and to the need "to create and extend an enlightened public opinion in favour of the principles of the *People's Charter*", but at the end of the statement there is an extremely general reference, almost in the pre-industrial language of the Enlightenment, to "devoted servants in the cause of human liberty and social happiness". Yet, whereas the LWMA address had spoken generally of libraries of reference and useful information, the National Association address recommended carefully that the libraries should be of "a hundred to two hundred volumes each, containing the most useful works on politics, morals, the sciences, history, and such instructive and entertaining works as may generally be approved of." It also had a long new section on *Public Halls* or *Schools for the People* to be used in the daytime by children and in the evening by adults. The educational proposals were strongly influenced by Owen, although Lovett anticipated later rather than earlier thought on the organization of education when he propounded his firm conviction that "it is the duty of the Government to provide the means of educating the whole nation; for as the whole people are benefited by each individual's laudable exertions, so *all* ought to be united in affording the best means of developing the useful powers of each".

What is said about education in *Chartism; A New Organization of the People* is so extensive that Professor Tawney claimed that the book as a whole was "an educational tract rather than a political manifesto". Yet this is, perhaps, a somewhat misleading way of putting it. Lovett had always believed that education mattered

profoundly both to working men in their struggles and to
society as a whole if it were to progress. In his own life he
had ample experience of "the hawks and owls of society
seeking to perpetuate the state of mental darkness". He
did not separate education from politics. "The reflecting
portion of our brethren", he wrote confidently in his
Preface, "are beginning to perceive the great necessity
for this intellectual and moral preparation;—not as set
forth by those 'educationists' who seek to spread their
own exclusive or sectarian notions, or by those who seek
to train up the youthful mind of our country to be
submissive admirers of 'things as they are'; but for
establishing such a just and extensive system of education
as shall ere long make our country intellectually great,
politically free and socially happy." The instrument was
related directly to its objects.

It is important to relate Lovett's "plan" for education,
which included infant, preparatory and high schools,
teachers' training schools and agricultural and industrial
schools for orphans, to his ideas about "the benefits of
organization". What was at stake was "effective union,
efficient political power, with knowledge and virtue to
use it for your children's welfare, so that freedom and
happiness may be perpetuated among them". The "plan"
could be financed, he believed, on the very simple basis
of every one who had signed the Chartist Petition contributing a penny a week or even a shilling a quarter. On
the latter calculation, 80 District Halls or normal
industrial schools, costing £3,000 each, could be built
each year, along with 710 circulating libraries, four
missionaries could be employed and 20,000 tracts a week
circulated. Such financing would be a proof of will: "the
best test of every man's political principles is not what he
will *profess* but *what he will do* for the cause". There
would be immense side advantages also. Political discussion and association would be strengthened immediately, while there could be sure knowledge that long-term
gains would be accruing all the time. Democratic
management would itself be a means to achieve
democracy. "With a people so trained, exclusive power,

corruption, and injustice would soon cease to have an existence."

There is no doubt of the enthusiasm that Lovett felt for his own plan. He had learned enough from his earlier activities to envisage it in national terms: "we must feel an equal interest in the *political enlightenment* of the most distant and indifferent inhabitant of our island as in that of our nearest and best disposed neighbour". It was easy for him to pass from the simplicity of its general ideas to detailed descriptions of what precisely should be taught and how it should be taught, and his book included meticulous illustrations and ended characteristically with "specimens of lesson cards". Unfortunately for him, it is doubtful whether many of the people who considered his "plan" ever got to that point in the argument, an often abstract argument which introduced no names of people and no concessions to those who felt, for whatever reason, that politics centred on something more than reasoned and reasonable study, debate and discussion. He admitted that "the passions of the multitude are frequently God's messengers to teach their oppressors justice", but he never tried to stir people's passions himself. The drama of politics he always despised.

As soon as his book was published, and he had made his first efforts to implement its provisions, it was attacked without restraint in the *Northern Star* and on Chartist platforms. "*Education* was ridiculed", Lovett complained, "*Knowledge* was sneered at, *Facts* were perverted, *Truth* suppressed, and the lowest passions and prejudices of the multitude were appealed to, to obtain a clamourous verdict against us." Lovett was always most eloquent when he was protesting angrily against personal attacks made upon him. "Believing themselves supremely wise," he wrote on this occasion of his enemies, "they spurn with Gothic ferocity all knowledge, truth, or justice; and, judging from their actions, they seem to think that liberty can only be realised by violence and prescription." He looked forward eagerly, if thoughtfully, to the time when "Gothic ferocity" would disappear: indeed, he believed that education would dispel it. There was nothing "romantic" in his view of present, past or future.

Committed as he was to politics, Lovett was no politician. His "plan" had less popular appeal than O'Connor's land plan which was based on far more rickety finance and offered little long-term hope. The year 1841 saw a general election when issues different from those which interested Lovett were being urged at the hustings, and the year 1842 was a dark year in British history, a year of hunger and despair, when Chartists were drawn into other urgent struggles. Lovett became the Director of a District Hall, erected according to his own prescription, but he soon learned, even if he was slow to admit it, that "integrity, purity, firmness, zeal and benevolence", qualities which were singled out in a testimonial presented to him in 1848, were not enough to guarantee social change. Even when educational change came belatedly later in the century, it was not along the lines he had advocated. Yet it is important to note that he was never alone in proclaiming the message set out in *Chartism; A New Organization of the People.* Once more Hetherington, Cleave and Watson joined him in the new Association, which had its own short-lived journal, *The National Association Gazette.* Like him, they believed that "a mantle of oblivion should be cast over past differences" and that "the wise and good of all classes" had to unite "to follow and reason together to work out the social and political regeneration of man".

Although it seems that Lovett, like Owen earlier, had reached an *impasse* during the 1840s, what happened to him was part of a pattern. To understand the pattern, it is necessary to turn to other lives, and to other parts of the nineteenth century. There was as big a gulf between Cobbett and Lovett as there was between Lovett and O'Connor, and Lovett's own career, distinctive though it was, had much in common with that of other self-taught men of his generation. Henry Hetherington, "the Demosthenes of the West", as his admirers called him, was caught up in similar, if less systematic and more romantic preoccupations. An early Chartist missionary and, like Lovett, a determined advocate of working-class temperance, he spent two years in gaol for his Chartist activities; and the "Newport Rising" of 1840, one of the few episodes in Chartist history where physical force was deliberately used, was based on an attempt to free him from gaol. On his release from gaol he was to announce that in his view "the days of idle bombast and rank are gone by". He was disliked by O'Connor at least as much as Lovett was, and he, for his part, attacked, like Lovett, "knaves and fools, who never earnestly desired the political emancipation of the working classes, but merely the gratification of their own vain frippery or their own egotism, their own buffoonery and their own demagogical tendencies". Like Lovett, he believed in "the raising of Halls in which members may meet for the acquisition of Political, Moral and Scientific Information". He diverged from Lovett, however, as he became increasingly involved in new agitations strongly supported by middle-class interests, and acquired a post-Chartist reputation as an itinerant lecturer. His correspondence with Place shows that he was willing to put more reliance not only on the middle classes but on Place than Lovett ever did. His approach to politics led towards popular mid-Victorian liberalism.

Vincent's career was paralleled in many respects by that of Robert Lowery, the Chartist of the North-East, who described *Chartism; A New Organization of the People* as "one of the most comprehensive and practical plans for elevating the working men which has ever yet been offered to the public". He supported Lovett's "New Move", but went on to associate himself, like Vincent, with the temperance movement and other social causes which he believed reconciled or might reconcile class antagonisms. He found many allies among ex-Chartists. There had been many Chartists in Scotland, for example, who emphasized the same points even when they did not favour an "alliance" with the middle classes. "We may not be producing great effects upon the Government," the *Scottish Patriot* exclaimed in December 1840, "but we are forming a character for the people which they have never before possessed—making them intelligent by instruction and moral by inculcating the principles of total abstinence." A. G. O'Neill, who moved from Scotland to Birmingham in 1840, was an eloquent advocate of the same philosophy. It was Collins who first invited him to Birmingham, and at a Birmingham meeting of "three hundred and fifty well dressed and most orderly conducted working men and their wives" held to honour Collins in October 1841 O'Neill insisted that "no beneficial revolution could be effected in this country which was not based on the moral and intellectual culture of the people".

O'Neill, unlike Vincent but like Lovett, was opposed to such a degree of dependence on middle-class support that working-class independence was jeopardized or, as Lovett would have put it in old age, the independence of those individuals who belonged to the working class. The problem of class relations never lost its relevance as both Cobbett and O'Connor faded into history. In understanding the close structural relationship between the stormy history of the 1840s and the intricately entangled history of the 1850s and 1860s, it is interesting to note two points about Lovett's career. First, the first person to offer Lovett a job after his release from gaol was Samuel Smiles, then editor of the *Leeds Times*—a less surprising link than it would have appeared before recent re-evaluations of Smiles. Self-help and mutual help were seldom poles apart. Much in mid-Victorian England had roots in Chartist experience. Second, and equally important, Lovett, as the century went by and the country grew less turbulent, never repented of his own past. "Most of the reforms that have taken place in my day", he wrote at the end of his life, "have been won rather in despite of the wealthy and titled classes than owe to them their origin, though they might at least have been made the unwilling instruments for carrying them into effect. . . . The industrious classes, therefore, would do well . . . to resolve to do their work themselves."

Asa Briggs

A note on further reading

There is no satisfactory single-volume narrative history of Chartism. M. Hovell's *The Chartist Movement* (1925) remains, with many weaknesses, the most useful. The earliest contemporary account, M. Gammage's *History of the Chartist Movement* (1854), is still worth reading. So too is T. Carlyle's *Chartism* (1839).

There have been many recent studies of Chartism, however, which enable it to be understood more clearly. The volume of essays *Chartist Studies* (ed. Asa Briggs, 1959) represents collective scholarship concerned mainly with local Chartist movements, their differences and how they were related to each other. The recent historiography has been examined by F. C. Mather in a Historical Association pamphlet, *Chartism* (1965). The best Chartist biography—of Harney, a Chartist very different from Lovett—is A. R. Schoyen, *The Chartist Challenge* (1956). To understand perspectives, E. P. Thompson's *The Making of the English Working Class* (Penguin edn., 1968) is indispensable.

Lovett lacks an adequate biography. The best source is still his book *The Life and Struggles of William Lovett*, first published in 1876. There is an abbreviated reprint (1967), with an out-of-date introduction by Professor Tawney written in 1920. One article is indispensable on the background of those Chartists who in some respects were not unlike Lovett—B. Harrison and P. Hollis's 'Chartism, Liberalism and the life of Robert Lowery' in the *English Historical Review*, Vol. LXXXII (1967). See also J. F. C. Harrison, *Learning and Living, 1790-1860* (1961).

BIBLIOGRAPHICAL NOTE

The first edition of *Chartism; A New Organization of the People*, "written in Warwick Gaol, by William Lovett, cabinet-maker, and John Collins, tool-maker", was published in London in 1840 by J. Watson, H. Hetherington and J. Cleave. This edition is reprinted in the present volume.

A second edition, incorporating minor alterations and additions, was published in 1841. To the names of the original publishers was added that of W. Lovett. In his autobiography, *The Life and Struggles of William Lovett*, published in 1876, the author states that the first edition "having been very favourably reviewed by the Press, we were induced, in consequence, to stereotype the second edition; but this not selling (in consequence of the clamour subsequently raised against us by the O'Connorites) caused us to lose by the transaction."

J. L. Madden

A DESIGN FOR A DISTRICT HALL.

CHARTISM;

A NEW ORGANIZATION OF THE PEOPLE,

EMBRACING A PLAN FOR THE

EDUCATION AND IMPROVEMENT OF THE PEOPLE, POLITICALLY AND SOCIALLY;

ADDRESSED TO THE WORKING-CLASSES OF THE UNITED KINGDOM, AND MORE
ESPECIALLY TO THE ADVOCATES OF THE RIGHTS AND LIBERTIES OF THE
WHOLE PEOPLE AS SET FORTH IN THE " PEOPLE'S CHARTER."

WRITTEN IN WARWICK GAOL,

BY

WILLIAM LOVETT, CABINET-MAKER,

AND

JOHN COLLINS, TOOL-MAKER.

———————

London:

J. WATSON, 15, CITY ROAD, FINSBURY;
H. HETHERINGTON, 126, STRAND; AND J. CLEAVE,
1, SHOE LANE, FLEET STREET.

1840.

PREFACE.

Being desirous of exerting the humble abilities God has given us towards procuring for our brethren *equality of political rights*, and placing them in such a *social condition* as shall best develope and preserve all their faculties, physical, moral, and intellectual, we have presumed to put forth the following pages for their consideration, containing our opinions of the best means of accomplishing those important objects. Believing that the proposed act of parliament, entitled "The People's Charter," is calculated to secure *to all classes of society their just share of political power*, and forming one of the most important steps to all *social improvement*, we are desirous of seeing the energies of all *peacefully* concentrated to cause that measure to be enacted as one of the laws of our country. Unhappily, the conflicting opinions entertained by some portion of the working-classes regarding *the means* of accomplishing that object have hitherto greatly retarded it; but we trust that experience, the great teacher of mankind, has led them to perceive that no other means are likely to be so effective as *a peaceful combination of the millions*, founding their hopes on the might and influence of *intellectual* and *moral progress*. Our feelings, at least, being in favour of such a description of organization, have induced us to set forth the advantages it would possess;—*first*, in causing great numbers to join us who are politically indifferent, or entertain erroneous notions respecting the objects and intentions of "the Chartists;" and, *second*, of the mode of perfecting that union when formed, and preparing our brethren to enjoy all the *social* advantages of the political power they are now seeking to obtain. The reflecting portion of our brethren are beginning to perceive the great necessity for this intellectual and moral preparation ;— not as set forth by those " educationists" who seek to spread their own exclusive or sectarian notions, or by those who seek to train up the youthful mind of our country to be submissive admirers of " things as they are ;" but for establishing such a just and extensive system of education as shall ere long make our country intellectually great, politically free, and socially happy. Various propositions have been made at different times *for educating the whole people*, none of which have been, nor deserve to be, adopted, on account of their exclusive or sectarian character. There is also so much evil to be apprehended from placing the education of our children in the hands of any government, especially of an *irresponsible one*, that it becomes one of the most important duties of the working and middle classes, to take the subject into their own hands, and to establish a just and liberal system of education, lest the power of educating their own children be taken from them by the arbitrary act of a corrupt and exclusive government. If, therefore, we should succeed in arousing the attention of the millions to the great importance of the subjects treated of in this pamphlet, we think we shall not have suffered twelve months' imprisonment in vain.

CONTENTS.

———

	Page.
PREFACE	iii
Introduction	1
Proposed Rules and Regulations for the National Association of the United Kingdom......................	24
Ground Plan of a District Hall	42
Benefits of Organization	44
Importance of General Education, and the Modes to be pursued in the different Schools	63
Specimens of Lesson Cards	112

INTRODUCTION.

THE spirit which has awakened, pervades, and moves the multitude, is that of intellectual inquiry. The light of thought is illuming the minds of the masses; kindled by the cheap publications, the discussions, missionaries, and meetings of the last ten years: a light which no power can extinguish, nor control its vivifying influence. For the spark once struck is inextinguishable, and will go on extending and radiating with increasing power; thought will generate thought; and each illumined mind will become a centre for the enlightenment of thousands, till the effulgent blaze penetrates every cranny of corruption, and scare selfishness and injustice from their seats of power. *Chartism* is an emanation of this spirit: its aim is the regeneration of all, the subjugation of none; its objects, as righteous as those of its opponents are wicked and unjust, are to place our institutions on the basis of justice, to secure labour its reward and merit its fruits, and to purify the heart and rectify the conduct of all, by knowledge, morality, and love of freedom. Discord and folly have to some extent unhappily prevailed, for want of sufficient investigation, but still Chartism has already been led by knowledge beyond the crushing influence of irresponsible and vindictive persecutors; and though prejudice and faction may contend with it for a season, it is yet destined to become a great and efficient instrument of moral and intellectual improvement.

It will be well, therefore, for all those who seek the happiness and prosperity of their country—who seek to enjoy the fruits of honest industry, to extend their hands and exercise their hearts in acts of benevolence and humanity—to make wiser preparations to meet this growing spirit than are advised in the arming proclamations, and found in the acts of whiggery. Our rulers may exasperate by coercion, but they will find it powerless in conquering the minds and subduing the hearts of the millions; of men who, tracing their burthens to exclusive legislation, are determined to obtain their just share of political right *at any sacrifice*. Those who madly rule the destinies of England may adopt the same policy their equally insane predecessors pursued towards unhappy Ireland; and like them may succeed in widening the gulph between rich and poor, and severing those feelings of justice and humanity which ought to unite man with his brother man. They may extend their blue-coated *gend'armiere* from town to village; they may fortify with soldiery every workshop, and convert the peaceful hills and dales of England into one great arsenal, to keep the haughty and extravagant few in possession of unjust power and domination: but in the maddened attempt they will throw back the rolling tide of intellectual and civilizing refinement; they will generate a military, suspicious, cunning, and vindictive spirit in the people, which, with taxation, oppression, want, and misery, will afford abundant materials for the storm of a frenzied and desolating revolution.

But will the spirit of Christianity, philosophy, and justice permit of these results? Will those whose active charity has caused them to explore, midst dangers and death, the remotest tent and wildest glen to instruct the mind and humanize the savage heart, forbear to exercise their benevolence in favour of their care-worn brethren at home? Shall Christian eloquence be employed against every species of slavery, but such as is found in the fields, the factories, and workshops of Britain? Will those who esteem all mankind as "brethren, and all the nations of the earth as one great family"—whose golden rules of Christian duty are based on principles of brotherly love, equality, and justice, permit these glorious principles to be outraged by men of wealth and power, merely because they profess to tolerate the teaching of principles they once persecuted and still scorn to practise? Will the followers of him who ever denounced extortion and injustice, and proclaimed that the poor and oppressed were *the especial objects of his mission*, remain silent spectators of oppression and injustice? Will the teachers and preachers of his inspired precepts be so far forgetful of their duty, as to side with the exclusive and oppressive few, whose ambitious projects and mercenary designs have converted earth's fruitful blessings and man's happiness into the curses of war, destruction, and misery?—with men who, not satisfied with *the black record of the last hundred and fifty years of blood and human wretchedness*, the curse of which still crushes us to earth,* are still pursuing the steps of their fathers, in warring against the rights and liberties of humanity?

	£
* The war of 1688 lasted *nine years,* and cost, at the time	36,000,000
Borrowed to support it, twenty millions, the interest on which, in one hundred and fifty-two years, at three and a half per cent, amounts to† .	106,400,000
The war of the Spanish succession lasted *eleven years,* and cost	62,500,000
Borrowed to support it, thirty-two and a half millions: the interest, in one hundred and twenty-seven years, amounts to	144,462,500
The Spanish war, ending in 1748, lasted *nine years,* and cost	54,000,000
Borrowed to support it, twenty-nine millions: the interest, in one hundred and two years, amounts to .	103,530,000
The war of 1756 lasted *seven years,* and cost .	112,000,000
Borrowed to support it, sixty millions: the interest, in seventy-seven years, amounts to . .	161,700,000
The American war lasted *eight years,* and cost . .	136,000,000
Borrowed to support it, one hundred and four millions: the interest, in sixty-five years, amounts to .	236,600,000
The French revolutionary war lasted *nine years,* and cost . . . , . .	464,000,000
Borrowed to support it, two hundred and one millions: the interest, in thirty-eight years, amounts to .	267,330,000
The war against Buonaparte lasted *twelve years,* and cost	1,159,000,000
Borrowed to support it, three hundred and eighty-eight millions: the interest, in twenty-five years, amounts to	339,500,000
	£3,383,022,500

To which amount must be added the increase of army, navy, civil list, half-pay, pensions, &c., which, within the above period, have been enormous; the value of British merchant vessels and their cargoes captured and destroyed, or wrecked by being deprived by those wars from access to friendly ports; and the enormous sums raised by poor-rates and charity which have been applied to mitigate the calamities those horrible wars have occasioned.

† The lowest rate of interest has been computed, and that from the conclusion of the war.

Can Christians read of those scenes of blood and carnage which exclusive legislation has engendered without horror? Can their imagination depict the fraudulent means by which fathers, husbands, and brothers have been torn from their families and homes, to bleed and die midst hecatombs of victims, without feeling the virtuous desire to remove *the unholy and brutalizing cause?* But these, say the advocates of exclusiveness, are the acts of days past, of scenes conscientiously lamented, and never to be renewed by any government. Friends of peace and humanity, trust not these deceitful boasters; hug not the specious deception to your hearts, but rather let the violated rights, the burning cottages, the slain, unburied, brute-devoured victims in Canada be their answers. Nay, refer them to ominous truths nearer home, and let the formidable answers to our supplications for "*justice*," in the shape of rifle-brigades, mortars, rockets, aud bludgeon men, convince you of the *improved feelings* of exclusive and class legislation.

The black catalogue of recorded crimes which all history developes, joined to the glaring and oppressive acts of every day's experience, must convince every reflective mind that *irresponsible power*, vested in one man or in a class of men, is the fruitful source of every crime. For men so circumstanced, having no curb to the desires which power and dominion occasion, pursue an intoxicating and expensive career, regardless of the toiling beings who, under forms of law, are robbed to support their insatiable extravagance. The objects of their cruelty may lift up their voices in vain against their oppressors, for their moral faculties having lost the wholesome check of public opinion, they become callous to the supplications of their victims.

Irresponsible, except to their own order, and equally extravagant and regardless, are those who now hold the

The estimated number of British alone slain or perished in the war ending in 1697	were	.	180,000
In the war which began in 1702	——	.	250,000
In the war which began in 1739	——	.	240,000
In the war which began in 1756	——	.	250,000
In the American war in 1775	——	.	200,000
In the French war began in 1793	——	.	700,000

The above note has been compiled from various sources.

political power of England. The working classes, therefore, having long felt the evils resulting from this irresponsible authority, in the *partial* laws they have enacted and unjustly executed, in the *partial* and over-
burthening taxation they have imposed upon them, and
in the insolence of those who live on the plunder they
have exacted, seek to establish a wholesome and RE-
SPONSIBLE GOVERNMENT, such as shall develope the energies and promote the happiness *of all classes in the state.*

And it remains to be seen whether the generous and
philanthropic minds with which our country abounds will
second these exertions. Whether those who are really
intent on reforming vice will perceive the necessity for
beginning *at the root of the evil*, having so often felt the
difficulty of improving the plant by merely trimming its
branches. And still more difficult will assuredly be their
efforts, morally and socially, to improve the people of
this country, while the present anomalous system of representation is permitted, with all its demoralizing influences. While we see vicious examples of bribery, fraud,
perjury, and intemperance held forth, in all their admitted
baseness and public notoriety, as means by which the
post of " honour" and seat of " justice" may be obtained;
thus sapping the very vitals of morality, by diverting the
aspiring minds of our country from the just and honest
pursuit of public estimation and public reward. While
by far the greater number of our legislators begin
their political career by the adoption of such unworthy
means, can we be surprised at the corrupt, unfeeling, and
often immoral conduct, so many of them display, or
wonder at the varied and multitudinous crudities they
dignify with the name of laws?

And when the effects of all these corrupting and pernicious influences are seen and felt throughout the length
and breadth of the land, engendering poverty, vice, and
crime, are we not justified in directing the public
mind to the attainment of *political reformation*, as the
most certain and direct means of all *moral* as of all *social*
reformation.

Can it any longer be doubted that ignorance and
poverty, springing from careless, extravagant, and vicious
rulers, originate the numerous and increasing demands
for our gaols, bridewells, penitentiaries, treadmills, and
other useless means of punishment, together with our

workhouses, asylums, and infirmaries—institutions which the want of proper education and encouragement to industry and frugality occasion?

A considerable number of individuals may be found, who see and lament the evils referred to, and trace them to the source described, but are deterred from exerting themselves to effect the change we aim at, by the drunken and profligate examples they daily witness. While they are anxious to effect a radical reform in our institutions, and turn to contemplate the proposal of political equality—of trusting men of such demoralizing habits with the suffrage, they are too often led to conclude that the change would be the greater evil. But we would anxiously advise persons who have arrived at such conclusions, to review their facts and re-exercise their judgments; and, according to their sincerity, we think they will see just cause for changing their opinions. Have they satisfied themselves, in the first place, that the *majority* of drunken and vicious characters are not already in possession of the franchise? Else, what other reason can they assign for the extent of bribery and intemperance so prevalent at our elections; when the vicious propensities of those *who have votes to dispose* of are basely gratified, by men equally base and destitute of principle to administer to such servile and brutal appetites? But, granting that the soul-degrading vice of drunkenness is still too prevalent among the most ignorant of the working classes, what is the *political* injury that could possibly arise from giving them votes *under the provisions of the Charter?* Were the franchise, indeed, to be extended, and the present electoral arrangements preserved, the septennial act retained, and all the inducements for bribery afforded as at present; there might, indeed, be some chance of the circle of drunken voters being inconveniently enlarged, to the trouble and expense of those who purchase *a seven years' influence* in parliament to idemnify them for the outlay.

Nay, further, have those objectors to the rights of the industrious classes, on the plea of intemperance, examined the facts and evidence that from time to time have been published regarding *the source of the evil,* and still fail to perceive *its origin in the misgovernment of the people?*

When they learn that the mental and physical debility arising from protracted and excessive toil, begets a craving appetite for stimulants to assist them beyond (or to re-store) their natural powers, and find that wholesome and nutritious ones are not always within the reach or means of the poor; they must assuredly perceive that our social and political arrangements must be highly defective, to occasion such degrading results.

When they perceive the mass of the population toiling from youth to age like beasts of burthen, with little means or time for intellectual or moral improvement, debarred by cruel and vexatious laws from cheerful exercise or joy-ous recreations, and encouraged in the pernicious habit of drunkenness by the facilities which government holds out, in order to exact its revenue of FIFTEEN MILLIONS from the sale of intoxicating and poisonous ingredients, can they any longer doubt the *originating cause*, or fail to perceive that the best remedy will be a just government?

When, under all these social and political disadvan-tages, they find the spirit of temperance and sobriety per-vading the ranks of labour, daily diminishing the amount of drunkenness and dissipation—when they perceive an enlightened and inquiring mind generating other habits and feelings among them—when they see them struggling for political rights as means of improving their class and dignifying their country, can these objectors any longer refuse to aid them in their great and noble undertaking?

Are the patient, forbearing, hard-working population of Britain less qualified for freedom than are the working classes of Switzerland and America—countries where peace, industry, and property, bear conclusive evidence in favour of *Universal Suffrage?*

In the democratic cantons of Switzerland, agriculture and manufactures, being combined, produce prosperity in every cottage. Knowledge and Freedom, twin-sisters, have caused them to outspeed their neighbours in all the ingenuity and refinements of art. Their laws, based on equality, are few, just, and respected; customs, excise, and prohibitory laws, are banished from among them; justice, cheaply and impartially administered, is every man's protecting guardian; morality, intelligence, and comfort gladden every home; and when the most distant infringement on their rights has been threatened, the spirit of democratic freedom has warmed each heart and nerved each arm to guard them.

America, the home and refuge for the destitute of all

nations, is as prosperous as she is free. She is daily adding town to town and village to village, and making neighbours of her most distant population, by the most stupendous achievements of art. Her trade and commerce, increasing with her people, give abundance to industry; and idleness is nowhere respected for its pedigree among them. She has no debt to embarrass her industry or tame her spirit. Her taxes are few, and applied to the education and benefit of her people. For the last fifty years she has had poverty, prejudice, and vice transplanted from every clime to blend with her people and impede her progress. And notwithstanding all are allowed freely to share in her institutions, upon principles of equality, she has continued to select men for her presidents and rulers whose characters, conduct, and abilities, in peace or war, are rarely equalled and never surpassed. The only stain in her star-bespangled banner is that remnant of kingly dominion, *the slavery of her coloured population;* which, like its damning brother, *the infant slavery of England,* is more a feature of wealth and class domination, than of the spirit of her people or her democratic institutions. But in proportion as knowledge is extending its humanizing influence over the selfishness of wealth, and the power and prejudices created by its dominion, so is American slavery fast sinking to that oblivious pit, where all the impediments which now obstruct the happiness of *black* and *white* are destined to sink for ever.

Nor need the advocates of democratic government, as known in modern days, confine themselves to the two countries alluded to, for facts and illustrations in proof of its superiority over governments based on any other foundation. During the few years the democratic principle has prevailed in Norway, the rapid improvement and increased prosperity of her people, have shone forth the more conspicuously by the dark contrast afforded by her neighbour Sweden, a country blessed by nature with far greater means of happiness, but wanting the stimulating soul of freedom to convert them to the mental and physical uses of her people.

In Spain, a country blessed by God, and for ages cursed by the despotism of man—a country where plundering nobles and liberty-hating priests have bowed the people to the dust—even there, during the brief period of their popular constitution, their slumbering energies were awakened to generate industry, prosperity, and happiness, to which they were previously strangers, and which again vanished, when the liberty was crushed which first awakened them.

In fact, an example can scarcely be produced in modern history of any people, whose laws and institutions have been founded on *popular control*, without exhibiting distinguishing and beneficial results, above all others.

The opponents of democracy have not failed to collect the vices and follies of the *ancient republics*, and to display them in all their glaring inconsistencies before us, as so many proofs of the inefficiency and mischief of popular governments. But these ingenious sophists fail at the same time to point out a peculiar feature of modern democracy, which completely nullifies their argument; that feature is *popular representation*. By this great improvement in legislation numerous evils which were felt in the ancient democracies are avoided; for while every man can exercise his influence over his representative, to effect his political desires, the passions and prejudices of the multitude are kept back from the deliberations of legislation, or the decisions of justice. Under the *representative system*, the power of wealth and influence of oratory may exercise an indirect and pernicious influence in parliament; but their potent effects cannot, as in the assemblies of Greece, be brought directly to bear upon the people, whose decisions were oftener biassed by interest or feeling, than governed by reason. Moreover, when *antiquity* is referred to for examples descriptive of the general or political acts of the multitude, it should be remembered that our higher standard of morality, together with the art of printing and popularizing knowledge, have given advantages in favour of our population, so as to render such references useless by way of comparison.

But, viewing democracy under all forms, ancient or modern, and estimating its merits by the impulse it has given to intellect, morality, art, science, and all that contribute to the civilization of man, where are the results of kingly or aristocratical dominion that can outvie it in the contrast? True it is, that man may be goaded by coercion, or compelled by necessity, to beautify and enrich the land of his tyrants; but the most noble and enduring records of his power, *his intellectual and moral great-ness*, must spring from energies which freedom alone can awaken. Those splendid remains and ruins of kingly dominion, those monuments of human slavery and mind-less folly, which now stand in solitary and crumbling ma-jesty, are destined to fall and be forgotten; but the *moral* and *intellectual records* of Grecian and Roman freedom still exist in all their sterling and pristine excellence, min-gling with the laws, institutions, literature, and refine-ments of society, and will be carried down the stream of posterity, and continue to exercise their civilizing influ-ence when the hoary pyramids are crumbled into dust.

But what are the arguments adduced against our prin-ciples by our most decided opponents? or, rather, what are the groundless assertions their prejudices and fears have originated? The ancient and honourable institutions of England, say they, are the cause of her greatness; her power in peace—her success in war—her holy religion—her trade, commerce, and extensive dominion—all spring from "the harmonious government of King, Lords, and Commons."

That to uphold the power and dominion she has ac-quired, under these fostering influences, force has been necessary abroad and at home; offices of trust, service and rewards have had to be created, and "a *debt* neces-sarily contracted in providing all these requisites."

That the liquidation of that *debt* being as impossible as it would be imprudent, (seeing its numerous claimants add to the stability of the government,) "*its interest* must be punctually and honourably paid."

That to meet this annual *interest* of TWENTY-EIGHT MIL-LIONS, "*taxes* have been imposed to a burthensome though to a necessary extent."

That this great amount of *taxation* being severely felt by the middle and working classes, and strong feelings moreover being entertained by them against the established church, the army, the corruptions of the navy, and other necessary parts of our institutions; great danger is to be apprehended from any extension of the suffrage which "may give the masses a preponderating and injurious in-fluence in the Commons' House of Parliament."

That *Universal Suffrage* may give them this influence; and from their present deficiency of political information, united with their prejudices against our well-balanced

constitution, they are the more likely to be influenced by
violent and designing men, to destroy it altogether, and
consequently involve in that convulsion "titles, rank,
wealth, commerce, and all that constitute the pride and
glory of England."

Such is the *general tenor* of the arguments (openly or
enigmatically expressed) against the claims of the industrious classes, by the opposing factions of Whig and Tory.

Whether the "greatness" of England has emanated from
the clashing and opposing interests denominated a " well-
balanced constitution," or from her great natural resources and advantages, combined with the most enter-
prizing, skilful, and industrious population in the world,
is a question common sense observers may easily determine, especially if they take the history of our rulers in
one hand, and that of her people in the other.   So far
from agreeing with those *constitutional* admirers, in all
probability they would decide, that much of what is called
" greatness " is only insignificance and folly; and that THE
TRUE GREATNESS OF ENGLAND HAS ARISEN IN SPITE OF THE IG-
NORANCE, OBSTINACY, AND WICKEDNESS OF HER RULERS.—
Impartial observers might further determine, that the selfish ambition which caused our rulers *to war against the
rights and liberties of all nations, and to sacrifice every
principle of humanity and justice in extending our
colonial dominion*, the more effectually to obtain power
and wealth for themselves and their dependents ; is trea-
son against the God of justice, and arraign them as cul-
prits before his tribunal, for the blood they have spilt, and
the treasure they have wasted.   And therefore the enormous expenditure consequent on their atrocities, so far
from being called " national," should be designated " THE
BLACK RECORD OF EXCLUSIVE LEGISLATION."   That men in
power should so far practise on the credulity of a people
as to incur such a debt, and for such a purpose, still to go
on increasing it beyond all hopes of payment ; still to tax
and oppress them for its support, and transmit the burthen
to posterity ; and still endeavour to pursuade them of its
numerous advantages, will form a wonder without a
parallel in the world's history.   But inasmuch as these
men, together with their cunning and trafficing associates,
have succeeded in beguiling the *innocent*, the *friendless*,
and the *fatherless* into the belief that the " funded debt
of England" (this imaginative monster) is of all invest-

ments the most profitable and secure; and consequently have caused them to invest in it the savings of their industry, the provision for their children, and support for their old age; humanity and justice, being the great characteristics of Englishmen, will rise up *in any future legislature* to shield and protect such *victims* of our debt-contracting and liberty-destroying despots.

When the *"justice"* can be demonstrated of calling upon one man to support another man's religion; when tithes, pluralities, and high church debauchery can find *encouragement from scripture;* when standing armies in peace, and navies useless for war, present *better uses* than resting places for noble and gentle fledgelings; when *true* merit presents its claims, and *real* service applies for reward, and when none but the *useful* and *necessary* expenditure of our government is presented to a British public;—the church, army, and navy, will meet their reward, and have little to apprehend from popular prejudice or popular suffrage.—Those strange apprehensions which certain persons feel from the people's desire to be admitted in *their own Parliament House,* and, according to their old "constitutional right," manage and economise the national expenditure, would seem to indicate troubled and guilty consciences. Else why these dreadful forebodings about the people managing *their own affairs?*

According to the "Constitution," the Commons' House belongs to the *common people.* History informs us, that, at different periods, they have adopted different modes of choosing it, from *Universal Suffrage** to that of individual choice; and if they find their present mode an improper one, they have surely a right to change it for a better, without the interference of those who belong to the other parts of the Constitution. If those they once elected as *servants* have gradually assumed the mastery, and by the power they were first invested with have rendered the People's House a corrupt and subservient instrument for party and faction to plunder and oppress the industrious with impunity, it is indeed time to talk of radical reform, in order that *the people's portion of the Constitution* may be placed in its original position, fairly to "balance" all the others. But if those sticklers for our Constitution,

* See a series of interesting articles on this subject in the Charter Newspaper, signed "*Revolutionist.*"

who are industriously opposing the efforts now making to *reform* the House of Commons, fail to recognize in their reading of that Constitution the right of Universal Suffrage ; it will remain for them to prove *its great and superior excellence to the satisfaction of the multitude.* And great must be their ingenuity if, in these inquiring times, they can persuade them that universal labour and universal taxation do not fully entitle them to Universal Suffrage.

The supposition that Universal Suffrage would give the working classes a *preponderating power* in the House of Commons, is not borne out by the experience of other countries. They are far from possessing such a power even in America, where wealth and rank have far less influence than with us, and where the exercise of the suffrage for more than half a century have given them opportunities to get their rights better represented than they are. But *wealth* with them, as with us, will always maintain *an undue influence,* till the people are *morally* and *politically* instructed ; then, indeed, will wealth secure *its just and proper influence,* and not, as at present, stand in opposition to the claims of industry, intellect, merit, freedom, and happiness. But the great advantages of the suffrage in the interim will be these : it will afford the people general and superior *means* of instruction ; it will awaken and concentrate human intellect to remove the evils of social life ; and will compel the representatives of the people to redress grievances, improve laws, and provide means of happiness in proportion to the enlightened desires of public opinion. Such indeed are the results we anticipate from the passing of the PEOPLE'S CHARTER.

The assumption that the working classes would elect "violent and designing men" is equally absurd and groundless, as their public conduct on several occasions testifies. For, setting aside, as altogether worthless, the idea our opponents entertain, that all who differ from them in politics are " violent and designing," we maintain that, taking into account the whole of the political or municipal contests of the last seven years, the candidates who have been elected by the multitude by a *shew of hands,* have been better qualified for their respective offices, both *intellectually* and *morally,* than those who were subsequently elected by the *privileged class* of voters. It would be invidious were we to mention names, and draw parallels in proof of this assertion; but if any man of unbiassed mind will contrast the cases that have come within the range of his experience during that period, he will agree with its general correctness. Whether such discrimination in working men betrays the "want of political information," and proves the superior mental qualification of electors, can only be partially proved, and that by examining the *meritorious* acts of the successful candidates. It would be well, however, if those who taunt the industrious classes with their "political ignorance," had first reviewed their political struggles during the last ten or twelve years. If they had considered their efforts to establish the rights of free discussion, to open mechanics' institutions, establish reading rooms and libraries, form working men's associations, and others of a like character; and, above all, their sufferings and difficulties in establishing a cheap press, by which millions of periodicals are weekly diffusing their enlightening influences throughout the empire; and then, if those scoffers at the ignorance of the millions had considered their present efforts to obtain their political rights, we think they would have reserved their illiberal taunts for others than the working classes. True it is that *individual exceptions* among the middle and upper classes have meritoriously assisted in all those efforts; but the energies, sufferings, and pence of the working classes mainly effected those glorious triumphs. The aristocracy, for the most part, have ever been active persecutors of all political improvement; and the middle classes, too intent on buying, selling, and speculating, have remained apathetic or sneering spectators of the efforts of the many; till success showed the prospect of advantage, and patronage appeared profitable.

It is further said, that considerable doubts are entertained of the propriety of trusting the working classes with power, lest they use it to the prejudice of *rank* and *property*, and the injury of our *institutions*. But what foundation is there for such doubts? In what country of the world are the rights of property more respected? Where are there more laws to guard it, and where are such laws more easily enforced, than in England? In fact, the patient submission to arbitrary and *unjust laws* for securing property (laws in opposition to their constitutional rights), constitute the weakness of Englishmen. When property has been threatened by foreign foe or domestic spoiler, who have been more forward to defend or active to guard it, than the calumniated and unprotected sons of labour? Petty spoilers exist in every country, but the grand enemies and violators of property in England are to be found among the enemies of the labourer. Corrupt and blundering politicians, gambling fundholders, speculating tricksters in trade and commerce, these are the great violators of the rights of property; men who, by one specious act or knavish trick, swamp the prosperity of millions, and convert in a moment the most enlivening prospects of industry to the desolation of despair. But even in those convulsions of ignorance or fraud, who are keener sufferers than the working classes? or who have had more useful experience to convince them of the necessity of property being fixed on the firmest foundations, than those whose homes of comfort have been rendered miserable by those political or commercial panics? Where, too, are the claims of merit or the legitimate influence of rank better appreciated than with us? or where are the efforts of humanity and benevolence better supported and encouraged than among the labouring population of England? Then away with those ungenerous surmises, those fears and anxieties respecting them. *Their interests are blended with the interests of property*, and they have sufficient good sense to perceive it—their hopes of happiness are based on the prosperity of their country, and all and everything appertaining to individuals, to classes, to our laws or institutions which can in any way be promotive of general prosperity, will ever be held sacred and inviolate by the industrious and generous hearted people of Great Britain and Ireland.

But, say some of our most captious and prejudiced opponents, while there is some truth in these observations regarding the general disposition and feelings of the working classes if they were left to their own unbiassed judgments, an exception must be made to that mischievous and discontented party who, under the names of "Reformers," "Radicals," and "Chartists," are actively engaged in spreading dangerous opinions among the people, and exciting them to acts of violence, incendiarism, and revolution. Now, as we belong to this very "discontented party," and plead guilty to the title of "Chartist," and are as active too as our humble abilities permit in propagating what the enemies of truth call "dangerous opinions;" yet we beg to disclaim on behalf of Chartists *generally* the charge of "*violence and incendiarism.*" The term "revolutionary" may be very appropriate in characterising all effectual reforms.—But what proofs of " violence or incendiarism" have they to adduce against *the great body of the Chartists?* unless, indeed, like Warwickshire juries, they find their verdict on one case by the facts of another. A few individuals may certainly be found in different parts of the country, whose feelings or sympathies have at times got the better of their judgments, and prompted them to talk violently or behave unjustly; and others from very different motives may have committed very illegal and wicked acts; but we hold it to be equally as unjust to condemn the great body of Chartists for such acts, as it would be to condemn the whole of the aristocracy or any other class of persons, because bad men have frequently been found among them. But such conduct would appear to be a part of the tactics of our opponents, in order to afford a pretext for prosecution, and to scare the timid and unreflecting from our ranks. It has been customary, time immemorial, for the advocates of injustice and gainers by corruption to impugn the motives and execrate the name of every man who, sympathising with his brethren, has been induced to step out of their ranks to make known their grievances and embody their feelings in the language of truth. And the time has been when such daring conduct has met with torture and death. The progress of opinion has, however, limited the power of despotism; and slander, persecution, and imprisonment are the modern instruments for stifling grievances, and checking the progress of truth. If, however, those persons to whom fate has consigned the destinies of government ever profited by experience, it might be supposed that they had had already sufficient to convince them of the fallacy of such persecuting efforts. It is true they may crush victim after victim, and by reeking swords and revengeful laws strike back one timid adherent after another, in the vain attempt to keep back just principles; but the energies and sympathies God has implanted in the human mind will ever cause such principles to be fostered, and will ever embolden new advocates to extend their dominion. But corrupt and selfish rulers seldom reason on future consequences; they have hitherto been blindly permitted to cut through every obstacle by force, to add injustice to the misery they create, and thus transmit new difficulties to their successors. Happy would it be however for posterity, if all those who are seeking to promote the happiness of mankind raised their voices against such monstrous injustice, and, instead of siding with unjust governors, investigated the claims of the governed. Had this been done towards the Chartists, or had even those men who *professed* the principles of Chartism before they were combined in a definite and practical form, been true to their professions, and put themselves, as they ought, in front of the public will they helped to create, much of the bitterness of feeling and violence of language which disappointment and distrust occasioned would have been spared, and, ere now, one of the most important of triumphs achieved in favour of human liberty.

What, let it be asked, are the claims of the Chartists? what is their character? and who are the men so designated? Are their claims unjust? are they unreasonable? are their characters depraved? are they men dangerous to the welfare and happiness of society? Let all those uninterested in the corruptions of the present system ask those questions; let them examine carefully, investigate impartially; and Chartism will soon have additional defenders. They will find their claims to be based on just, scriptural, and constitutional foundations. They will find their principles ably set forth in the annals of whiggery, and vindicated by the most eloquent and talented of British statesmen. And if the most active and reflecting portion of our population, the most temperate and industrious, and the most earnest in their desire to see justice substituted for oppression, truth for falsehood, and knowledge for ignorance, have any claims of character the reverse of depravity, then such investigators would find that Chartism and the character of the Chartists have been grossly misrepresented; for of the majority of such characters are their ranks composed. Doubtlessly they are not free, any more than other bodies, from individuals who are prompted by vain, ambitious, or interested motives; nor are they all equally temperate in language or action; but of this we are certain, from our intimate knowledge of the working classes, that the Chartists are the *elite* of that class, both intellectually and morally, and are influenced by the most generous and disinterested desire to promote the happiness of their fellow-men. Their general character must not be estimated by individual or isolated cases of violence or folly. They have often been deceived themselves by the high-sounding professions of individuals both *within and without* St. Stephen's; and when they have seen their most humble supplications scoffed at and disregarded, a different or a louder tone must not be set down to their prejudice. In fact, the experience of the past would seem to indicate that the passions of the multitude are frequently God's messengers to teach their oppressors justice; for when they have spurned alike reason and argument, they have often yielded to passion what they have refused to sober justice. There is little hope, however, that our modern rulers will improve upon the old; but if all those truly benevolent minds who are labouring earnestly to improve the condition of the multitude, would carry their investigations to the root of our political and social evils—would separate themselves from corrupt oppressors, and unite with those of the industrious classes who are in pursuit of the same object as themselves; they would find the great body of the Chartists the most efficient instruments that could be desired in carrying forward all the beneficial reforms contemplated; and the Chartists, in return, animated by such co-operation, would prove the most zealous, temperate, and powerful auxiliaries in banishing intemperance, poverty, and crime, and in raising the intellectual and moral character of the people beyond the expectations of the most sanguine philanthropist.

But, fellow-workmen, while we ought to be anxious for the co-operation of good men among all classes, we should mainly rely on our own energies to effect our own freedom. For if we fail in activity, perseverance, and watchful exertions, and supinely trust our liberties to others, our disappointment will remind us of our folly, and new burthens and restrictions place our hopes at a still greater distance. Benevolent and well-intentioned individuals of all classes have warmly espoused our principles, and have zealously laboured to extend them; and thousands, we trust, will yet be found equally ardent and effective. But when we consider the various influences of rank, wealth, and station, which are continually operating to deter all those above our own sphere from becoming the open and daring advocates of our rights; and consider, moreover, the numerous links of relationship, professions, business-connection, interest, and friendship, which bind them to our present system ; we should be the more readily convinced of the necessity of *self-reliance*, and the more firmly resolved by the concentration of every mental and moral energy nature has given us, TO BUILD UP THE SACRED TEMPLE OF OUR OWN LIBERTIES. The means are within our grasp, if we judiciously apply them, and no power on earth can prevent the consummation of so glorious an achievement. Then shall we the better appreciate what we have intellectually and morally erected; then shall we stand on its threshold erect, and enter its precincts rejoicing—possessing rights and feelings which no earthly power can confer, and inspired with a mental devotedness to use them for our country's welfare. And when we shall be no more, then may our children proudly point to that edifice raised by their hard-working progenitors when they were depressed by poverty, weakened by toil, and cursed by corrupt and plundering oppressors. Let our hopes then be built on our own united exertions, and let those exertions be proportioned to the magnitude of our object, and success will soon yield us a bountiful reward.

In proportion to our earnestness and perseverance will our numbers be extended, will our resources and influence increase, and will men of all ranks find it to be their interests to advocate the principles they now spurn, and to associate with the men they now stigmatize and persecute.

Unquestionably a superficial consideration of the exertions we have made and the disappointments we have experienced, during the last three or four years, is too apt to dispirit us. For, while lamenting our poverty and complaining of our burthens, we have seen one oppressive project after another introduced into parliament, supported by those we thought our friends, and eventually carried by large majorities. We have exhausted reason and argument to show the injustice of such measures, and have prayed and supplicated in vain against their enactment. Finding our rights and interests daily sacrificed by such conduct, we sought a share in the making of the laws we were called upon to obey. We availed ourselves of the constitutional usages of our country, we met in millions, and peaceably petitioned for redress. While our complaints were disregarded, our arguments exasperated and our numbers excited the terror of our oppressors. Hence, every delusive scheme was invented to check the progress of our principles, and every species of force employed to silence the voice of our advocates. The right of public meeting was invaded by despotic mandates, and a new system of espionage adopted to control our boasted freedom of speech and liberty of action. In fact, every means that our rulers could devise and their minions execute, have been adopted to keep us in social and political bondage.

But, fellow-countrymen, while the recollection of such injustice may cast a momentary cloud across our hopes, the voice of duty should arouse us to redouble our exertions in a cause so noble as the one we have espoused. If we remain in apathy, be assured that the misery of the Irish peasant will be our lot or that of our offspring ; for, as certain as *the demon of misrule* has withered the energies and drained out the vitals of that unfortunate country, so will it drive out British capital by its taxation, monopolies, and oppression ; and, by drying up the resources of labour, break down and extinguish our middle-class population, and reduce us to such degradation and wretchedness as in all ages have ever followed the track of unjust government and corrupt spoilers. But if we stand forward as a band of brothers, linked in the cause of benevolence and justice, and resolve, at any sacrifice, to avert a fate so miserable to ourselves and posterity, our *numbers*, our *resources*, and *combined operations*, will surely reward us with success.

But, then, it may be asked, what other form of combination, what other means than those we have already employed, can be adopted to accomplish our political and social salvation ? Must we again spend our pence and breath *in useless prayers for justice ?* Must we, whose industry sustains the state, and whose arms defend it, *humbly* crave our rights from those who profit by our wrongs, and get rewarded for our servility with bludgeons and sabres ? Fellow-countrymen, while these last questions have occupied our most serious attention, we cannot recommend the repetition of such useless and hopeless labours. The most important questions that, we conceive, have engaged our attention during the last twelve months are these :—How can we best create and extend an enlightened public opinion in favour of the People's Charter, such as shall *peaceably* cause its enactment ; and how shall that opinion be *morally and politically trained and concentrated,* so as to realize ALL THE SOCIAL HAPPINESS that *can be made* to result from the powers and energies of representative democracy? While we have no disposition to renew the unwise and unprofitable discussion regarding "moral" and "physical" force; and while we maintain that the people have the *same right* to employ similar means to regain their liberties, as have been used to enslave them, we are anxious, as we have ever been, to effect our object *in peace.* And though we incurred no small share of censure from the most ardent of our brethren, for contending for the superiority of our moral energies over our physical abilities, we think the disposition we evinced, and the part we performed, both in and out of the Convention, towards carrying *all and every righteous measure* into effect likely to promote the passing of the Charter, will sufficiently exonerate us from any charge of cowardice, as well as from any selfish predilection in favour of our own opinions. And, however we may regret, we are not disposed to condemn, the confident reliance many of our brethren placed on their physical resources, nor complain of the strong feelings they manifested against us, and all who differed in opinion from them. We are now satisfied that many of them experience more acute sufferings, and daily witness worse scenes of wretchedness, than sudden death can possibly inflict, or battle-strife disclose to them. For, what worse can those experience on earth who, from earliest morn to latest night, are toiling in misery, yet starving while they toil—who, possessing all the anxieties of fond parents, cannot satisfy their children with bread—who, susceptible of every domestic affection, perceive their hearths desolate, and little ones neglected, while the wives of their bosoms are exhausting every toiling faculty in the field or workshop, to add to the scanty portion which merely serves to protract their lives of care-worn wretchedness? Men thus steeped in misery, and standing on the very verge of existence, cannot philosophise on prudence; they are disposed to risk their lives on any chance which offers the prospect of immediate relief, as the only means of rendering life supportable, or helping them to escape death in its most agonizing forms. When we further reflect on the circumstances which have hitherto influenced the great mass of mankind, we are not surprised at the feeling that prevails in favour of physical force. When we consider their early education—their school-book heroes—their historical records of military and naval renown—their idolized warriors of sea and land—their prayers for conquest, and thanksgivings for victories—and the effect of all these influences to expand their combative faculties, and weaken their moral powers, we need not wonder that men generally place so much reliance on physical force, and undervalue the superior force of their reason and moral energies. Experience, however, will eventually dispel this delusion, and will cause reformers to hold in reserve the exercise of the former, till the latter has been proved to be ineffectual. Nor can we help entertaining the opinion, that recent experience has greatly served to lessen the faith of the most sanguine in their theory of force, and caused them to review proposals they once spurned as visionary and contemptible. While we never doubted the constitutional right of Englishmen to possess "arms," we have doubted the propriety of placing reliance on such means for effecting our freedom; and further reflection has convinced us, that far more effective and certain means are within our reach.

Thus far we have deemed it necessary to explain our views on this point, and now let us cast the mantle of oblivion over all past follies and by-gone dissensions; we have one great object in view, and *must be one in soul to achieve it*. We have suffered persecution for that object, but have not been convinced of the justice of our enemies—we have been crushed with severity, but our spirits have not been broken—calumny has assailed our cause, but has failed to lessen our attachment to it—the triumph of our principles has been delayed, but it will not be the less certain. But, fellow-countrymen, in order to ensure this speedily, we should endeavour, in the first place, to satisfy ourselves as to *the most efficient kind of combination*, and then direct all our energies to its accomplishment. And in this pursuit we must avoid all contentious feelings, and carefully and calmly consider the different propositions that may be submitted for our consideration. With this desire, we respectfully submit that our combination should be such as to induce all those to join us who are sincerely interested in the social and political improvement of the millions—such as shall render us the most efficient aid to effect these objects, while it places us in the best possible position to enforce our political claims—and such as in our progress will afford ourselves and children the means of superior education, so that permanent benefits and substantial fruits may result from our labours. As some persons, however, may imagine that such important results are not within the compass of practicability, while others may suppose that the numerous objects embraced in such a plan are calculated to place our political emancipation at a greater distance, we proceed at once to submit the following " Plan, Rules, and Regulations," for the consideration of our brethren; hoping we shall hereafter be able to demonstrate its practicability, and prove it to be *the nearest means* towards the accomplishment of our great object—that of securing to all men THEIR EQUAL POLITICAL AND SOCIAL RIGHTS.

PROPOSED

PLAN, RULES, AND REGULATIONS

OF AN ASSOCIATION, TO BE ENTITLED,

THE NATIONAL ASSOCIATION

OF THE

UNITED KINGDOM,

For Promoting the Political and Social Improvement of the People.

———

WHILE general or local associations are not wanting for extending in charity the dogmas and exclusiveness of sects, or proclaiming the ostentatiousness of pride—for spreading knowledge and sympathy abroad, while both are greatly needed at home—for the mitigation of the physical and mental ills of life, while the originating causes are neglected—for the acquisition of languages, literature, and professional skill—for refining the tastes and enriching the imaginations of mankind—for investigating the properties of all nature, from the most minute object to the most stupendous—and for rendering the powers and uses of every element subservient to the production of wealth ; there seems to be wanting an association paramount in importance to all—ONE FOR POLITICALLY AND SOCIALLY IMPROVING THE PEOPLE. To supply this great national deficiency, it is proposed that an association be established, and that the following be its objects :

First. To unite, in one general body, persons of all CREEDS, CLASSES, and OPINIONS, who are desirous to promote the political and social improvement of the people.

Second. To create and extend an enlightened public opinion in favour of the principles of the PEOPLE'S CHARTER, and by every just means secure its enactment ; so that the industrious classes may be placed in possession of the franchise, the most important step to all political and social reformation.

Third. To erect PUBLIC HALLS or SCHOOLS FOR THE PEOPLE throughout the kingdom, upon the most approved principles, and in such districts as may be necessary. Such halls to be used during the day as INFANT, PRE-PARATORY, and HIGH SCHOOLS, in which the children shall be educated on the most approved plans the association can devise; embracing physical, mental, moral, and political instruction;—and used of an evening for PUBLIC LECTURES, on physical, moral, and political science; for READINGS, DIS-CUSSIONS, MUSICAL ENTERTAINMENTS, DANCING, and such other healthful and rational recreations as may serve to instruct and cheer the industrious classes after their hours of toil, *and prevent the formation* of vicious and intoxicating habits. Such halls to have two commodious play-grounds, and, where practicable, a pleasure garden, attached to each; apartments for the teachers, rooms for hot and cold baths, for a small museum, a laboratory and general workshop, where the children may be taught experiments in science, as well as the first principles of the most use-ful trades.

Fourth. To establish, in such towns or districts as may be found necessary, NORMAL or TEACHERS' SCHOOLS, for the purpose of instructing schoolmasters and mistresses in the most approved systems of physical, mental, moral, and political training.

Fifth. To establish, on the most approved system, such AGRICULTURAL and INDUSTRIAL SCHOOLS as may be re-quired, for the education and support of *the orphan children of the association*, and for instructing them in some useful trade or occupation.

Sixth. To establish CIRCULATING LIBRARIES, from a hun-dred to two hundred volumes each, containing the most use-ful works on politics, morals, the sciences, history, and such instructive and entertaining works as may be generally approved of. Such libraries to vary as much as possible from each other, and to be *sent in rotation* from one town or village in the district to another; there to be placed in the hands of a responsible person, to be lent out according to the rules, and, after a stated time, forwarded to the next district.

Seventh. To print, from time to time, such TRACTS and PAMPHLETS as the association may consider necessary for promoting its objects, and, when its organization is complete, to publish a monthly or quarterly national periodical.

Eighth. To offer premiums, whenever it may be considered advisable, for the best essays on the instruction of children; for the best description of school-books for infants, juveniles, and adults; or for any other object promotive of the social and political welfare of the people.

Ninth. To appoint as many MISSIONARIES as may be deemed necessary, to visit the different districts of the kingdom, *for the purposes of explaining the views of the association*, for promoting its efficient organization, for lecturing on its different objects, for visiting the different schools when erected, and otherwise seeing that the intentions of the general body are carried into effect in the several localities, according to the instructions they may receive from the general board.

Tenth. To devise, from time to time, the best means by which the members in their several localities may collect subscriptions and donations in aid of the above objects, may manage the superintendence of the halls and schools of their respective districts, may have due control over all the affairs of the association, and share in all its advantages, without incurring personal risk, or violating the laws of the country.

RULES.

———

OFFICERS OF THE ASSOCIATION.

THE affairs of this association shall be conducted by a general board of management, a president, vice-president, treasurer, secretary, and such sub-committees and assistants as may be found necessary.

GENERAL BOARD—HOW CHOSEN.

Every county possessing *five hundred members of this association* shall be privileged to elect *one* member to the general board of management; and if possessing more than twice that number, may elect *two* members, but no more. Their election shall take place in the month of May in each year, in the following manner:—A public meeting of all the members of the association within the county shall be called, by public advertisement, for the purpose of electing a member or members of the general board, of which meeting six days' notice shall be given. On the day of meeting, after the proposers, seconders, and candidates have explained their views, the voting shall commence, and the votes be collected as follows: As many balloting boxes as may be found necessary shall be placed in different parts of the meeting, each box having as many partitions as there are candidates (or one box for each, if found more convenient); and on the top and front of each partition shall be legibly affixed the names of the respective candidates. Two scrutineers shall be appointed by each candidate to stand by each balloting place, to see that none but persons qualified do vote, and that the voting is conducted fairly. The members of the association shall then vote *with their cards of the last quarter*, and them only (and persons unwell or residing at a distance may send their cards, and empower their friends to vote for them)'; which cards they shall drop into the partitions of their favourite candidates, through a slit on the top of each partition.* After it has been publicly announced from the hustings that the balloting is about to be closed, and a further reasonable time allowed for all members present to vote, the balloting shall cease. The boxes shall then be sealed, and taken away to the first convenient place, where, in the presence of the candidates, or their friends, the scrutineers shall count the votes. After which they shall at once proceed to the hustings, and publicly announce the names and numbers of the respective candidates, and declare the persons who are elected.

OFFICERS—HOW CHOSEN.

The president, vice-president, treasurer, secretary, and such other officers as may be required, shall be elected *by the general board* on the first day of its sittings in each year; the election shall be by ballot, and decided by a majority of votes. All members of the association (whether elected to the general board or not) shall be eligible to fill any office according to their competency.

MEMBERS—THEIR ELIGIBILITY.

All persons, *male* and *female*, approving of the objects, and conforming to the rules of the association, are eligible to become members, *and share in all its advantages*, on paying in advance the sum of *one shilling* for a card—the same *to be renewed every quarter*.

THE PRESIDENT—HIS DUTIES.

It shall be the duty of the president to attend all meetings of the general board, and preside over their deliberations. He shall see that all questions are discussed consecutively, according to the notices given; that no member speak more than once on the same question, unless in reply; and that proper order and decorum be preserved. He shall sign all official orders or documents passed by the board, as well as all money orders voted by

---

* If there are two members to be elected, the cards may be torn in two.

them, or commissioned by their authority. He shall be empowered to order an especial meeting of the board to be summoned on any extraordinary occasion, as well as to order a meeting of the officers of the association to be called, whenever he may deem it necessary.

THE VICE-PRESIDENT—HIS DUTIES.

During the time the president is present, the vice-president shall assist in the business of the board, and when he is absent, shall preside over their deliberations. He shall also perform such other duties appertaining to the office of president as he may require of him under his written authority.

THE TREASURER—HIS DUTIES.

The treasurer shall cause all moneys received by him to pass through the hands of the bankers, and shall keep a correct account from their books of all moneys transmitted to them, and the names of the persons from whom sent. He shall pay all bills of the association under an order of the general board, and signed by the president or vice-president, but not otherwise. He shall see that all checks on the bankers are signed by himself and the president or vice-president. His accounts of receipts and expenditure shall be open for the inspection of the general board, and other officers of the association, whenever they meet; and every year he shall prepare a general balance-sheet, to be laid before the board the first day of its sittings.

THE SECRETARY—HIS DUTIES.

The secretary shall attend all meetings of the general board, as well as all meetings of the officers of the association, and keep correct minutes of their proceedings; which minutes he shall read over at the next meeting. He shall conduct all the correspondence of the association, and confer with its officers respecting all business of importance. He shall see that new cards are issued for the members *(of a different colour each quarter)*, and are forwarded to the members of the general board, as hereafter provided. All moneys, either subscriptions or donations, which pass into his hands, he shall hand over to the treasurer, and keep a correct account of the same, as well as of all petty cash he may have expended, and make out a balance-sheet of the same, to be laid before the general board the first day of its sittings.

MEMBERS OF THE GENERAL BOARD—THEIR DUTIES.

The members of the general board shall meet in London *the first Monday in June* in each year, for the transaction of business; they shall hold their sittings from day to day (Sunday excepted), but shall not prolong them beyond a fortnight; and in case an extraordinary meeting be convened by the president, their sittings shall not exceed that time. Their meetings shall be open to gentlemen of the press, and such members of the association as the room will accommodate. The expenses of the members of the board to and from London must be defrayed by the members of their respective counties. It shall also be their duty to receive, from the secretary, the new cards for the members every quarter; as well as to appoint responsible and proper persons to issue the same to members (or persons desirous of becoming members) in different parts of their respective counties. They shall keep a list of the names and residence of the persons they may so appoint, as well as a correct account of the cards they entrust to them for distribution. They shall also see that such persons do properly fill up the cards, and keep a correct list of the members who purchase them; so that the numbers not disposed of may be returned when required. It shall also be their duty to see that no cards are issued on credit, and that the receipts of those sold are returned to them before they send out the cards of the next quarter. At the commencement of every quarter they shall cause all sums in their possession to be transmitted to the bankers of the association in the names of the treasurer, president, and vice-president for the time being; and at the same time send the particulars to the secretary, who, on ascertaining that the money is received, shall transmit them a receipt. They shall be paid the postages of all letters and carriages of all parcels by the treasurer of the association.

SUB-COMMITTEE—THEIR DUTIES.

The president, vice-president, treasurer, and secretary, for the time being, together with such members of the general board as choose to attend, shall be considered a perpetual sub-committee *when the board is not sitting.* They shall meet every three months, or oftener if required, for the purpose of performing such business as may be necessary, their powers having been previously defined by the general board.

THE MISSIONARIES—THEIR DUTIES.

The missionaries shall be appointed by the general board, at a weekly salary, *out of which they shall pay all the expenses of their mission.* It shall be their duty to visit such places and perform such duties as the board may require, according to a plan of their route and written instructions they shall receive. It shall be their especial duty to perfect the organization of the association in each county they may be called upon to visit, to explain its objects and advantages, to visit the different schools, see that the books and tracts of the association are properly circulated, and that its rules are everywhere properly observed. They shall be supplied by the association with placards for calling such meetings as may be required, together with tracts for distribution, and cards and rules, if necessary.

COUNTIES TO BE DIVIDED INTO DISTRICTS.

In order to divide the different counties into districts, according to such numbers of the association in each as would render the erection of a hall and establishment of schools useful, it shall be the duty of the members of the general board to call a general meeting, on *the first of October in each year*, of all the persons they have appointed to issue members' cards in different parts of their respective counties. The persons so assembled in each county shall determine the number of districts in *their* county, according to the number of paying members, which shall be denominated hall districts. They shall then make out a proper list of such districts, which, having been signed by the chairman of the meeting, and five others, shall be forwarded to the secretary of the association, for purposes hereafter mentioned.

THE ERECTION OF DISTRICT HALLS.

At the annual meeting of the general board, they shall determine, according to the funds in the hands of the bankers, how many district halls shall be erected; and in order that the funds may be usefully and justly apportioned, the following plan shall be adopted:—The *names of all the counties* in which there are five hundred members of the association shall be written on as many different slips of paper, which slips shall be carefully folded and put into a balloting box properly constructed for the purpose. A person shall then be called into the room, and requested to draw out as many of the said slips as it has been previously resolved to erect halls; the names on which slips shall be the counties in which they shall be erected. The counties having been so determined on, *the names of the districts* in each *successful* county shall be written on similar slips of paper, and each county separately balloted for in like manner; the last drawn slip in each county shall be the district in which the hall shall be erected. As soon as the balloting is concluded, the secretary shall write to each of the successful districts, requesting them to call a general meeting of the members of the association residing in the district, for the purpose of electing *twelve proper persons for superintending the erection of the hall, and for its management when erected*, as well as *seven trustees*, in whose names the property shall be invested in trust for the benefit of the district, according to rules and regulations which the general board shall provide for those several purposes. It shall also be the duty of the association to appoint a qualified person to see that the hall is erected in accordance with its plans and objects; but if any additional sum be added by the subscriptions or donations of the district, such sums may be applied to beautify or enlarge it in any manner, so long as the original design be complied with.

NORMAL SCHOOLS.

In order to provide such schools as the association may establish with efficient teachers, it shall be the duty of the general board to establish, as soon as possible, such normal schools (with model schools attached to them) as may be required. They shall found them in such places, and on such rules and regulations, as in their judgment will best promote the objects of the association. They shall also see that such normal schools are provided with proper school-teachers or directors, and supplied with the best works on physical, mental, moral, and political training; as well as such school apparatus as will best serve to perfect the teachers in the art of properly training the rising generation. The rules referred to shall declare the qualifications for admitting persons to be instructed as teachers, and after they have studied the time required by the rules, and have been declared fully competent by the directors, they shall be provided with *credentials of the association attesting the same;* and after a sufficient number of such teachers are properly qualified, none shall be employed in the schools of the association but those provided with such certificates.

AGRICULTURAL AND INDUSTRIAL SCHOOLS.

It shall be the duty of the general board to establish (as soon as their funds will enable them) such agricultural and industrial schools as may be found necessary for the educating, supporting, and instructing in some useful trade or occupation *the orphan children of the association.* They shall be established on the most approved plans, and in such situations as the board may consider desirable, and shall be provided with such efficient means of instruction and support as shall hereafter be set forth in the rules and regulations of the association.

SUPERINTENDENTS TO BE ANNUALLY ELECTED.

After the first election of the superintendents of the halls and schools as before provided for, an annual election of them shall take place in the month of July in each year, in the following manner :—The old superintendents (or any twenty members, if they refuse), shall cause a notice to be stuck on the front of the hall door a fortnight previous to the election, announcing the time when and place where the meeting of the members of the district shall take place for the purpose of electing twelve superintendents for the next year, and stating the time when all nominations must be given in. Lists of the persons so nominated shall then be printed, and one be sent to each of the members, who shall mark off on the list *the twelve persons he or she approves of ;* and on the day of the meeting shall drop such list in a box made for that purpose. Four scrutineers shall then be appointed to examine such lists, and declare who are the persons elected. The superintendents of the last year shall be eligible to be re-elected.

RESIGNATIONS OR DEATHS.

On the resignation or death of any member of the general board, his place shall be filled up in the same manner as is pursued at a general election; excepting that the members shall be supplied with voting tickets instead of their quarterly cards. On the resignation or death of any general officer of the association, his place shall be filled up or supplied by the sub-committee, till the next meeting of the general board. And on the resignation or death of any district superintendent, the duties shall be performed by his colleagues till the next annual election.

ALTERATION OF RULES.

Any member of the general board desirous of proposing any alteration or amendment in the rules and regulations of the association, shall give two days' notice of the same, and the alteration be determined on by a majority of votes.

RULES FOR THE CIRCULATING LIBRARIES.

The general board shall determine, from time to time, the number of circulating libraries, and the description of books, that shall be provided in conformity with the objects of the association.

The case for each library shall be fitted up with moveable partitions, and so constructed as to form a strong box when shut, and (by hinging it in the centre of the back) a book-case when open.

The books in each case shall be properly numbered, and a catalogue and rules enclosed in each case, which shall be fastened with a lock and key.

The district teachers shall be the librarians, and in the event of there being none in a district, the members of the association therein shall select responsible persons to act as librarians, and shall send the names of such persons to the secretary of the association.

The general sub-committee shall cause the libraries to be sent *in rotation to the different counties;* and the librarians shall send them in rotation *to the several districts in each county.*

Each library shall be retained in a district *three months;* and when the arrangements of the association will permit, *four libraries shall be sent to each district every year.*

The expenses of conveyance to the several counties shall be paid by the association, and the expense from district to district by the members of each; all fines to be applied to that purpose.

The loss of any books, or injury of any library, shall be made good by the district in which such loss or injury occurs.

The books shall be lent out under the following regulations, or such others as may hereafter be found necessary.

The librarian shall issue any volume contained in the library to any *member* of the association *who produces a card of membership.*

No member shall have more than one volume at a time, nor keep it longer than one week; but any volume may be re-issued to the same person, if not bespoke.

If any member keeps a volume longer than a week, he or she shall pay a fine of one halfpenny per day for every day above that time.

If any book already issued shall be bespoke by a member, that member shall have it next.

Any member injuring a volume shall pay such reasonable fine as the district superintendents shall require.

Any person *not a member* may be allowed the use of the library, on leaving the value of the volume in the hands of the librarian, and by paying *a penny for each volume.*

The librarian shall keep an account of all the receipts and fines of the library, which shall be open for the inspection of the members, and applied as before mentioned.

RULES FOR THE HALLS.

The district halls shall be erected on such plans as the *general board* may conceive best calculated to promote the objects of the association.

Each hall shall be fitted up and furnished with such seats, tables, desks, school-apparatus, and other requisites, as may be necessary, at the expense of the association.

Every district hall, when erected, shall be invested in the names of such trustees as the members of the association residing in the district may think proper to elect, and *be legally secured for their benefit, and that of the working classes of the district, for all future time.*

The officers of the association shall also provide, by every legal means in their power, that such halls be hereafter devoted to the purposes originally intended, and as declared by their rules and objects.

The sole management and superintendence of the hall and schools shall be in the power of the *twelve superintendents* for the time being.

The superintendents shall be elected *annually*, as provided by the rules of the association, but may be removed for misconduct or neglect of duty ; the same to be decided at a general meeting of the members of the district, called for that purpose.

The trustees shall have no other power or control in the management than such as is vested in them by the title-deeds, unless they are appointed superintendents as well.

It shall be the duty of the superintendents to see that the hall is applied to such purposes as are declared in the objects of the association, and that its rules and regulations are properly enforced.

At any general meeting of the members of the district, they may make such bye-laws as they may consider necessary for the regulation of the hall, for the furnishing the museum, laboratory, and workshop, and for the management of the baths, but they must not contravene the laws and objects of the association ; such *bye-laws* to be enforced by the superintendents.

The superintendents may let out the hall (at any time when not required by the members) for any object promotive of the welfare of the people ; the proceeds to be applied to the purposes of the hall or schools.

Every member on entering the hall shall be compelled to show his or her *quarterly card ;* and none but members shall be admitted, unless by such bye-laws or regulations as may have been previously agreed on by the members.

Any member wilfully violating any general rule, regulation, or bye-law, may be expelled the association by a vote of the members belonging to the district, at a general meeting called to investigate such conduct.

The great object of the association being to advance the social happiness and political dignity of the people of the United Kingdom, and intoxication being one of the greatest obstacles to that end, it shall be the especial duty of the superintendents to see that all intoxicating drinks are carefully excluded from the hall, school, playgrounds, or garden adjoining, as well as from all public meetings, festivals, and entertainments of the members. Nor shall the hall, rooms, or grounds adjoining, be let to any parties, for any purpose, where intoxicating drinks shall be introduced.*

RULES FOR THE SCHOOLS.

Every district hall shall be constructed on such a plan as to have (in addition to its other apartments,) two lofty and spacious rooms, one above another, to serve the purposes of school-rooms during the day, and lecture, reading-rooms, &c., of an evening.

The lower room shall be used as an INFANT SCHOOL for boys and girls from three to six years of age; and the upper room as a PREPARATORY SCHOOL for children from six to nine, and HIGH SCHOOL for children from nine years of age and upwards, of both sexes. In all the schools the boys should sit on one side of the room, and the girls on the other.

Both school-rooms shall be fitted up on the most approved principles, and the arrangements in the upper room shall be such that the children of the high school shall be separated from those of the preparatory school. The upper room shall be furnished with tables instead of

---

* Arrangements might easily be made for procuring coffee, tea, ginger beer, lemonade, or any other refreshment, upon an economical scale.

writing-desks, and so constructed as to answer the purposes of the school, and that of the lectures, festivals, &c.

The play-grounds shall be fenced round, and a border round each of them shall be tastefully laid out with plants, flowers, and such fruit and other trees as may be suited to the locality. There shall also be such gymnastic arrangements made, as may be considered necessary for the exercise of the children. The play-ground on one side of the hall shall be for the children of the infant school, and that on the other for the children of the other schools. Whenever locality and circumstances will permit, a piece of ground shall be attached to the hall, for the purpose of teaching the children a knowledge of horticulture and gardening, as well as for the pleasure and amusement of the members of the association. No child under six years of age shall be admitted into the preparatory school until he has gone through the rudiments of the infant school, nor shall any pupil be admitted into the *high school* until he has been qualified by the instruction of the *preparatory school.*

The plan of education in all the schools shall be THE BEST THE GENERAL BOARD CAN DEVISE for giving the best physical, mental, moral, and political training to the children, so as to prepare them in strength, morality, and intellect, to enjoy their own existence, and to render the greatest amount of benefit to others.

In the INFANT SCHOOL *cleanliness and punctual attendance* should be scrupulously insisted upon, as one of the best means of amalgamating of class distinctions, and preserving the children from corrupting influences. The first object of the teachers should be to place the children in accordance with the laws of their organization. And it is doubtless in opposition to those laws to confine them in close atmospheres, drilled to sit in one posture for hours, and to have their little feelings operated upon by the fear of the rod, of confinement, and of all the numerous follies at present practised to compel submission. The *air and exercise* of the play-ground are the first essentials at this early stage, where their teachers should as carefully watch over them as in the school-room, and, when all their faculties are in full activity, infuse those principles of action, justice, and kindness, necessary to form their character, which at that age will be more impressive than book instruction. They should be taught a knowledge of *things* as well as of *words*, and have their properties and uses impressed on their senses by *the exhibition and explanation of objects*. Principles of morality should not be merely repeated by rote, but the why and wherefore familiarly explained to them; their leading precept and practice should be to " *love one another.*"

In the PREPARATORY SCHOOL the same habits of regularity and cleanliness should be enforced. They should, as best fitting to their physical developement, have sufficient time for healthful exercise and recreation. They should be carefully taught *the laws of their organization*, and the evils of infringing them; as forming the most important lessons to inculcate temperance in eating and drinking, and all their physical enjoyments. They should be equally taught the evils that are certain to arise to themselves and society from *the infringement of the moral laws of their nature*. It should be the duty of their teachers familiarly to acquaint them with the *social* and *political relations* that exist between them and their fellow-beings. They should be taught by the most simple explanations and experiments to perceive and discover the *use, property, and relationship of every object* within their own locality, and learn to express in *writing*, and in *correct language*, the ideas they have received. The use and principles of *arithmetic* should be taught them by the most simple methods. They should be taught to understand the principles and practice of *music*, a gratification and a solace even in the hut of poverty. Their *imagination* should be sedulously cultivated, by directing their attention to everything lovely, grand, or stupendous, around them; as affording a wholesome stimulus to greatness of mind, and a powerful antidote against the grovelling vices so prevalent in society. In fact, the end and object of their teachers should be the equal and judicious developement *of all their faculties*, and not the mere cultivation of the intellect.

The HIGH SCHOOL should be for the still higher developement of all those principles taught in the preparatory school. In addition to which the children should be taught a more extensive acquaintance with the *topography, resources, pursuits, and habits of the country they live in*, and with the *physical* and *natural phenomena of the globe they inhabit*. They should be instructed in the *principles of chemistry*, and its general application to the arts, trades, and pursuits they may hereafter be engaged in; in the principle of *design*, and its general utility in all their avocations; a general knowledge of geology and mineralogy, and their most useful application. With the variation required by sex, they should be taught the *first principles of the most useful trades and occupations* in the laboratory and workshop. In addition to which, if a portion of land be attached, they should be practically taught a knowledge of horticulture and gardening. They should be fully educated to love knowledge and morality for their own sakes, and prepared to go out into active life with sound practical information to direct them, and a moral stamina to withstand its numerous temptations.*

As the primary object of the association is to unite the members in one bond of brotherhood, the more effectually to secure their political and social welfare, to train up their children to appreciate the excellence of knowledge and virtue, the spirit of universal benevolence and mutual forbearance ought to prevail among them regarding all religious creeds and doctrines. And as the attempt to introduce *any particular forms of religion* would tend to create dissensions among them, and lead all those whose own views had not been adopted to be jealous and distrustful of those of others, the aim of the general board should be carefully to exclude from their system of education all such questions of dispute. That great precept of "*love one another*" should be the basis of their educational discipline, and *the moral and intellectual virtues* should be developed in the minds of the children, that their parents may perceive that more genuine Christian charity will result, than if their children were drilled to the constant reading of what they could scarcely comprehend, or in repeating precepts by rote without their importance being exemplified by practice. Surely, when abundant time can be found for imparting religious instruction beyond that dedicated to the school, and when so many religious instructors, of all denominations, can be found most willing to impart their peculiar opinions, it would seem to be more in accordance with the precepts of Christ, mutually to unite in morally educating our children *to dwell in peace and union*, which are the great

* A portion of the above outline, written by W. Lovett, was issued in an address on the subject of "National Education," by the Working Men's Association, about three years ago.

essentials of religion, than by our selfish desires and sectarian jealousies suffer ignorance, vice, and disunion to prevail.

Under the system of education adopted in the schools, *all corporeal punishments should be dispensed with,* as highly mischievous under every form, as they serve to call forth revengeful propensities in some, and cow others into slavish subjection. Reason may direct the intellect to see impropriety of conduct, and kindness subdue the feelings of anger; but blows and injudicious privations only strengthen a harsh disposition.

As the association, *in its infancy,* will not be able to render any pecuniary assistance towards supplying the districts with as many efficient teachers as it would be *desirable to retain* for the purposes of the schools, it will be necessary for each district to make such prudent arrangements, at first, as their means will enable them, till assistance can be afforded. *Two* QUALIFIED *teachers* (man and wife, if possible,) with two female assistants, will serve in the commencement for both rooms; and, when the arrangements of the association are complete, there should be two such qualified teachers, and one assistant to each school-room. The female teacher (if *qualified* in a normal school,) will, with a competent assistant, be able to manage the *infant school;* and the male teacher, with an assistant qualified to teach the girls in their sewing, knitting, cutting out their own clothing, &c., will serve at the commencement for the *upper schools.*

The teachers should be chosen *by the members of the district,* and the assistants *by the teachers,* subject to the approval of the superintendents.

The mode of admitting children to the schools, as well as their payments, ought to be decided by the members, and declared in their bye-laws ; but, while one of their objects should be to obtain *cheap* education for their children, they should remember that its *efficiency* will greatly depend on the talents and energies of the teachers and assistants; therefore their payments should be such as to procure for them a handsome and comfortable subsistence.

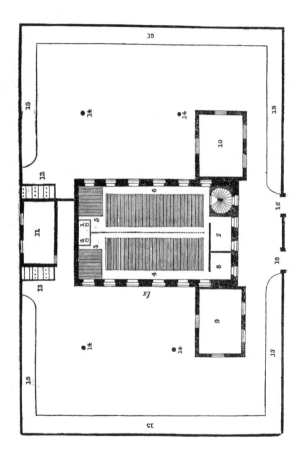

PLAN OF THE UPPER FLOOR OF THE HALL, &c.

1 The seat of the male teacher.
2 The seat of the assistant.
3 Girls of the high school.
4 Girls of the preparatory school.
5 Boys of the high school.
6 Boys of the preparatory school.
7 Boys' hat and coat room
8 Girls' bonnet and cloak room
9 The museum, with the baths underneath.

10 Sleeping room of the teacher, with sitting room underneath, &c.
11 Laboratory, with workshop underneath
12 Girls' closets.
13 Boys' closets.
14 Circular swings.
15 Flower borders, &c.
16 Entrances.
17 The site of the door in the infant school.

Fellow-countrymen, we have now laid before you, for your consideration, a PLAN which, if carried into effect, would, in our opinion, speedily secure our political and social rights; and, by training up our children in knowledge and virtue, place the liberties of our country on a basis corruption could not undermine, nor tyranny destroy. We have chosen to present you with its details in the form of RULES AND REGULATIONS, as conveying clearer and more concise ideas of our views than we could hope to convey in any other form. It now remains for us to point out to you the abundant means you have to carry such a plan into operation, and consequently to realize greater social and political advantages than have ever been attained by the working classes of any country —the advantages of *effective union, efficient political power, with knowledge and virtue to use it for your children's welfare, so that freedom and happiness may be perpetuated among them.*

Few persons, we think, will be disposed to doubt that there is any considerable number of the industrious classes who cannot afford the small pecuniary amount we have mentioned as necessary to constitute them members of the NATIONAL ASSOCIATION. We grant that exceptions may be found among them, persons to whom *a penny per week* would be an important sum; but from our knowledge of the working classes in general, we feel satisfied that where there is one so wretchedly situated as not to afford so trivial a sum towards the salvation of his country, or the education of his children, there are hundreds who waste twice that amount daily; by expending it on that which neither contributes to their health, their happiness, nor their freedom. But admitting that great numbers of our class are, either from prejudice or ignorance, altogether careless respecting their political rights or social obligations, and will not for some time render us any assistance; let us form our estimate for carrying this plan into effect from the numbers and professions of those Radical Reformers who from their position were free to sign the NATIONAL PETITION. And we have abundant evidence to convince us that vast numbers both among the middle and working clases, were so circumstanced that, if they had appended their signatures to that petition, it would have involved them and their families in ruin. The numbers, however, who did sign it were ONE MILLION TWO HUNDRED AND

EIGHTY-THREE THOUSAND ; these at *a penny per week* from each person would realize the sum of five thousand three hundred and forty-five pounds and upwards weekly. But we have estimated the payment of members for the National Association at *less* even than a penny per week, at only *a shilling a quarter* ; and we may reasonably conclude that those persons who, at the risk of losing their employment and connection, and in despite of all opposition, so far interested themselves in preparing and signing that petition, and in contributing to the support of their delegates, have the same earnest desire to follow up the great cause of their political and social salvation by enrolling themselves members of an association such as we have described. And when we further take into account the great personal advantages to be derived from belonging to such an association, apart from the great political and social objects of our pursuit—when the benefits of the halls, schools, and libraries are considered, they will supply additional reasons for forming our estimate from the numbers who signed that petition. Supposing, then, that such a number of members as signed it belonged to the NATIONAL ASSOCIATION, their payments at a shilling a quarter would produce AN ANNUAL SUM OF TWO HUNDRED AND FIFTY-SIX THOUSAND SIX HUNDRED POUNDS ! ! ! This amount would enable the association to effect *every year* the following important objects :—

	£
To erect eighty district halls, or normal or industrial schools, at £3000 each	240,000
To establish seven hundred and ten circulating libraries, at £20 for each	14,200
To employ four missionaries, (travelling expenses included) at £200 per annum	800
To circulate twenty thousand tracts *per week* at 15s. per thousand	780
For printing, postages, salaries, &c.	700
	£256,480
Leaving for incidental expenses	120
	£256,600

But then it might be urged against this calculation, that great numbers of persons signed the National Petition who would not contribute a shilling a quarter to support such an association; that thousands of men are to be found who talk loud and threaten fiercely on any political question that comes before them, but are silent and apathetic on all *pecuniary* propositions for promoting the object of their boastings. While there may be some truth in these assertions, we cannot readily believe that these persons are very numerous; for surely when men are convinced that their excessive toil, their scanty earnings, the wretchedness and injustice they daily experience, can all be traced *to corrupt and exclusive legislation*, they must also be convinced that a public opinion, extensive enough to effect a thorough reform, cannot be created *without money or personal sacrifices;* and as some persons must be prepared to make them, there are few *right-thinking, conscientious men* so mean as to expect political benefits, without contributing their mite and their exertions to obtain them. But if such mean and despicable adherents to our cause are to be found—men who, by their hollow professions and apparent sincerity, *seek to generate a spurious and fleeting public opinion*, they are far greater enemies to reform than its bitterest opponents—their hypocrisy serves to mislead men of honesty and principle, and gives the enemies of liberty new pretexts for new oppressions. Mere lukewarm professors, too, are of little use to any cause, but are absolutely mischievous to ours, as they deceive us by swelling our ranks with "men of straw." The cause of political and social reformation cannot exist by mere sentiment—there must be action to give it vitality; and if men were once thoroughly convinced that most of the evils of life are created by vicious institutions, and that all its solid enjoyments are to be realized by their purity and excellence, they would be as zealous to effect the desired change as to banish disease and misery from their dwellings, and fill them with means of happiness.

The best test of every man's political principles is not what he will *profess*, but *what he will do* for the cause. No man should excuse himself for lacking intellectual attainments, or great pecuniary resources; every man, however poor or humble, has means to forward it, if he be honestly and zealously disposed towards it. Isolated and divided, we are poor and powerless; but, banded together, *our aggregate pence* will enable us, as we have shown, to perform prodigies in the cause of liberty. And when the importance of such an association as we have described is calmly considered—when the trifling sum required to support it, and render all its objects practicable, is viewed in connection with similar sums many persons spend foolishly and uselessly in the course of a year, we are sanguine in our anticipations that the great body of the *Radicals*, at least, have sufficient political virtue to rally round such an association, whenever it is formed. We seek not to influence your *feelings*, fellow-countrymen, so much as *to awaken your judgment;* and therefore we wish you to consider whether there is any other form of combination likely to be so politically and socially effective, to enable us more readily to obtain Universal Suffrage, and all the principles of "the Charter," than that we have presented to your notice. There are no *political advantages* which the numbers, resources, or combined operations of any other form of association would afford, that would not be possessed in an eminent degree by the members of the NATIONAL ASSOCIATION. But then its great superiority over all others would be these;—it would not use its energies and resources in meeting and petitioning; it would not, year after year, be engaged in the only task of endeavouring to induce corruption to purify itself: but it would be gradually accumulating means of instruction and amusement, and devising sources of refined enjoyments to which the millions are strangers; it would be industriously employed in politically, intellectually, and morally training fathers, mothers, and children to know their rights and perform their duties; and with a people so trained, exclusive power, corruption, and injustice would soon cease to have an existence. Need we particularize the numerous advantages that would result from such an association, if the millions of the working classes alone performed their duty towards it? In the first place, the great benefits of the district halls *must be apparent to Radicals above all others*, as they experience greater difficulties than others to obtain places of meeting. Their political opinions generally render them so obnoxious to those in authority, that it is seldom they can obtain the use of public buildings; and the proprietors of public houses and private rooms are so completely in the power of *the great men of the town*, that they dare not, in many instances, let their rooms for radical purposes. And no later than last year the police of the metropolis were em-

ployed to go from one public house to another, to threaten
the proprietors with the loss of their licenses, if they let
their rooms to the Chartists; and doubtlessly the same
system is practised in other places. But even if these
difficulties did not exist, the *great expense* of private
rooms forms no trifling obstacle to the frequent meetings of the working classes. If they turn their attention
to the green fields, or to the *common* heritage their fore-
fathers possessed for their "folkmotes," their "tithe-
motes," and other public purposes, they are there met by
the law of trespass, the power of exclusion, and the opposition of all the *squirarchy* of the town. The right, therefore, of public meeting and free discussion being subject
to and controlled by such despotic influences, form additional reasons for the people having their own district
halls to meet in. It is true the working classes in some
towns do not labour under these disadvantages; some
have sufficient control over their authorities, and others
have places of meeting which already serve their purposes.
But we are satisfied that *these are the exceptions to the
evil;* and it should be remembered, that the little good
that can be effected with those advantages is neutralized
by the obstacles our brethren experience in other places.
There are towns, too, where the working classes are power-
fully assisted by the middle classes, and where they have
abundant means to erect their own hall, independently of
any association; but still no such exclusive advantage
ought to prevent them from assisting their brethren who
are differently situated. THERE IS NO POLITICAL GOOD TO BE
ACHIEVED BY A SPIRIT OF EXCLUSIVENESS. We must therefore *diffuse our means of knowledge;* we must feel an
equal interest in the *political enlightenment* of the most
distant and indifferent inhabitant of our island as in that
of our nearest and best disposed neighbour, as the political *ignorance* or *corruption* of the one is as fatal to freedom as is that of the other. We have too long been
playing the game of political selfishness; and hence it
is we have been contending in vain for our rights.
One town boasts of its public spirit and political knowledge; the people of one district esteem themselves politically superior to another; one part of the country prides
itself on its preparedness for freedom, and speaks with contempt of the apathy of another: and the result of this
contracted spirit is exhibited in one part of the country

counteracting the good effected by another. The well-populated and enlightened town, where two Liberals are triumphantly elected, has its votes neutralized by the petty borough where the light of political knowledge has never dawned, where votes are bought and freedom sold.

Let us in future, then, look beyond this useless system of setting up a Liberal here and there to be knocked down by Whigs or Tories ; let us seek to carry our principles into the camp of our opponents—*to instruct the dupes of those corrupt and plundering factions;*—and ere long the ignorant supporters of oppression and misrule will become zealous advocates of freedom. To effect this object, we must cast aside all those local and foolish prejudices which render nugatory most of our exertions : *our aim is the emancipation of all,* and *political enlightenment* one of our principal means to effect it. In assisting to erect halls in Ireland or in Wales, *we are as effectually promoting our own and our children's freedom as if we erected them in our own district.* Wherever they may be situated, all will be *politically* benefited, though it will depend on the chances of the ballot, whether we or our distant brethren will first enjoy the *social* advantages to be derived from them. But if, as we have shown, a trifling portion of the working classes can effect so much in *one year,* we may reasonably conclude that by union and perseverance they would soon be established throughout the kingdom. And there is little doubt but that *other classes would contribute to such laudable objects,* if the working classes were to show a disposition to begin the good work.

The advantages of the CIRCULATING LIBRARIES would exist independently of the halls ; and what man or woman, with a taste for reading, or the hearing of books read by their children, would think the pleasure dearly purchased with *less even than a penny a week* ? We have seen sufficient of country places to know the great difficulties of procuring books of any useful description, and that the expense is often beyond the means of working people ;— but by belonging to the National Association, (independently of other important benefits,) they would have the choice of hundreds of volumes in a year for the merest trifle. What lover, then, of his species can reflect without pleasurable sensations on the great political and social advantages that must eventually arise from the circulation of good and useful works throughout every district in the country? For, by combining the instructive with the entertaining—by bringing within the reach of the isolated cottager and country mechanic works they would never otherwise hear of, regarding the improvements in art, the discoveries in nature, the beauties of ancient writers, productions of modern literature, and the most useful and instructive of our political writers, habits of reading and reflection would be generated among them, their rights and duties appreciated, their tastes improved, their superstitions and prejudices eradicated; and they would become wiser, better, and happier members of the community.

The LECTURES on physical, moral, and political science would be a never-failing source of instruction: the great volume of nature presents such variety, beauty, utility, and perfection, that the *instructed mind* sees new objects for daily admiration and nightly reflection. For the want of that mental culture, how much of nature appears barren and cheerless, which otherwise would teem with fruitful and never-ending sources of delight! But, unhappily, the deficiency of this mental pleasure, this intellectual stimulus, is not the only loss, for the void is too often filled up with sensual and vicious gratifications, hurtful to the individual and prejudicial to society. To illumine such minds—to interest the young, and stimulate the mental energies of the adult, should be the especial object of the lectures; plain truths, clearly demonstrated and aptly applied—facts well attested, authentic evidence, and close reasoning—useful and interesting experiments, with their practical application—and, as far as possible, made clear by diagrams and pictorial representations, would bring conviction home to the most obtuse, and be found at all times the readiest mode of imparting information. After a hard day's toil it often happens that, when the mind has lost its energies for useful reading, it is stimulated and improved by oral discourses, lectures, and experiments.

The public READINGS might vary according to the tastes of the members, either for conveying political or moral information, or for improving them in the useful art of *correct reading*. For the latter purpose, one of the best modes we have seen adopted is the following:—A chairman having been appointed, the names of all those who are desirous of reading are written on slips of paper, folded up, and thrown into a hat or box opposite the chair. A list of select pieces in *prose and verse* (which are generally selected on the previous evening,) is then read over; and the chairman, having drawn out one of the slips, reads over the name, and calls upon the person to read any piece he chooses from the list. After the person has read, the chairman invites the criticisms of the company: those who feel their competency give their opinions, as brief as possible, and in a spirit to encourage improvement, regarding the person's manner, pronunciation, emphasis, &c. After which, another is called on in the same manner; though it is sometimes advisable to call on one person to prepare himself while another is reading. Independent of the improvements in reading which we have seen effected in a short period by this method, we believe it to be an excellent means for giving confidence to young persons, and preparing for public speaking.

The utility of public DISCUSSIONS on useful subjects, when properly conducted, is beyond estimation; for, independent of the facilities they afford for instructing men in the art of publicly imparting knowledge, instructing their fellows, and defending their rights, *discussion is the best touchstone of truth.* A man may spend a lifetime in reading and storing his mind with knowledge; but without subjecting his intellectual stores to the test of discussion, by which the sterling ore may be separated from the dross, he will continue to carry about with him *as of equal value,* false theories, romantic speculations, crudities, and conceits of every description. A man may possess great intellectual riches—he may comprehend all the mysteries of art and nature; but unless he cultivate the art of imparting his knowledge to his fellow-men, he lives, with all his knowledge, but for himself: he is in the intellectual world what the miser is in the social. He may plead his defects and his inability in vain; for if he employed but a small portion of his time in cultivating the art of public speaking or writing, he would soon become useful in proportion to his knowledge. In every country, especially where its institutions are founded on popular power or subject to its control, it becomes the duty of every man to cultivate the abilities God has given him, so that by speaking and writing he may preserve its liberties, by exposing private peculations and public wrong.

We are aware that strong feelings exist in many parts of the country against DANCING and MUSICAL ENTERTAINMENTS ; and it will be well to inquire whether those feelings are founded on reason or prejudice : if on reason, we should obey their dictates; but if on prejudice, we should pursue an onward course, regardless of the contracted notions of those whose views have no foundation in reason. First, as regards MUSICAL ENTERTAINMENTS, the great objection to them seems to be against a particular description of music, which the religious world has designated "*profane ;*" and it would seem that the profanity is not in the cheerfulness or peculiarity of tune—for they often adapt those of the most lively description to their own hymns and psalms : from which it would appear that the primary objection is in the *sentiment*, and not in the tune. Now, though it is admitted that many of our songs abound in foolish, ridiculous, unmeaning, and objectionable sentiments, which all men of sense will readily unite to condemn, and expel from all rational society, yet this should form no valid argument against the introduction of *songs of an opposite description* into our entertainments. We have in our language songs conveying sentiments of the most exalted description, inculcating the love of freedom, social and domestic happiness, giving great praise to good deeds, exalting virtue and condemning vice, and depicting in glowing language the beauties of earth and skies. Sentiments of such description generally excite the admiration of the most fastidious ; and surely their excellence cannot be depreciated by being conveyed in verse, and expressed in all the melodious witchery of the human voice. As music has an irresistible influence on all, and as the burst of joyous feeling generally gives forth its expression in song, *the sentiments of which greatly influence individual and national character*, it is not for man to war with nature, by attempting to stifle her expressions, but to *change and purify the sentiments* in which they are expressed.

Among the social recreations in which both sexes can participate, the exercise of DANCING seems pre-eminent : its lively and graceful evolutions, and healthful, spirit-stirring tendency, have ever rendered it a favourite amusement in all countries. Whence, then, have originated the objections against it? Surely there can be none against a description of exercise which most medical men agree is, of all others, the best for enlivening the spirits, and strengthening the muscles of the body! Nor is there any reasonable ground for supposing it more prejudicial to *morality* for both sexes to meet in the dance, than in any other public assembly. The virtue of either sex is not a whit secured by any fastidious exclusion from each other's society; nor is the moral character of youth any way preserved by denying them those cheerful and agreeable recreations congenial to their dispositions. The objections to badly ventilated rooms, late hours, bad characters, or improper conduct, should lie against those particulars, but not against dancing; for it by no means follows that these should be associated with the amusements and entertainments of our respective districts. The generality of people are so constituted as to seek, at times, cheerful society and lively enjoyments; and *it should be the great object of all reformers to prepare legitimate means for the gratification of these feelings, without allowing them to be exposed to vicious associations.* Many of those who frequent public-houses in their hours of relaxation, are not so much induced by the love of drink, as to spend their hours in cheerful society; and if places were provided *(unassociated with the means of intoxication)* where they could spend a pleasant and agreeable evening, we should have little cause for lamenting the prevalence of intemperance, and its demoralizing consequences.*

The advantages of HOT AND COLD BATHS being attached to such an establishment must be obvious. The difficulties our labouring population meet with in large towns and inland districts, in getting access to convenient bathing-places, are productive of more serious consequences than many persons imagine. We are told by medical men that the perspiration of the body, which is continually going on, causes a species of incrustation on the skin, which materially interferes with its functions, which, if not removed by frequent ablutions, occasions a weakness of body and de-

* Those who could not join in the dance might be amused with the games of chess and drafts, which are both rational and instructive; but cards, dice, and all kinds of gambling, should be scrupulously excluded.

pression of mind; and, further, that the evil is greatly
increased when persons have to work at dusty employ-
ments and in unhealthy atmospheres. Hot or cold bath-
ing, then, according to the state of the person's health
or constitution, will be found a great preservative of
health, independently of the habit of cleanliness it would
serve to generate. And when the great benefit of the
hot bath, in many kinds of disorder, is considered, its
importance will be still further appreciated.

The small MUSEUM we have referred to could be furnished in a short time by the collections and contributions
of the members; and in proportion as they progressed in
a knowledge of the productions of nature or art, so would
it engage their attention, and be a source of great pleasure to themselves and their children.

The LABORATORY would serve for scientific experiments
by the members in their leisure hours, as well as for the
instruction of the children; and the GENERAL WORKSHOP
would possess similar advantages in other respects.

How far the exertions of a few intelligent and active
MISSIONARIES, constantly engaged in propagating the principles of the association, are likely to be effective, may
be estimated, in some respects, by the good that has
already been effected by such means. Four or six persons, thoroughly acquainted with all its objects, political
and social, inspired with sufficient zeal for the cause, possessing business habits, and having a capacity for lecturing
on most of the important points we have referred to,
would soon effect a complete organization of the country,
and would do more in twelve months to create an enlightened public opinion in favour of our views, than
could be effected by any other means in thrice the time;
more especially so if we provided each of them with *tracts*,
to be distributed, *(at the rate of twenty thousand weekly,)*
containing explanations of our principles, as well as facts,
statements, and expositions, regarding our objects generally.

We have referred to the necessity of offering *premiums*,
from time to time, for the best essays on the instruction
of children, for the best description of school-books, and
for any other object likely to promote the social and political welfare of the people. Though much has been written
on the subject of education, we think that very little of
it has been to the purpose: most of the writers have

founded their systems on erroneous notions, and it is only within the last few years that anything approximating to truth or utility has been written. Believing the *science of education* (for as such we consider it) to be but *in its infancy*, we think that every means should be devised to induce men of intellect to devote their attention to a subject of such vital importance, and that for similar reasons they should be encouraged to prepare a better description of school-books than those in present use. The social and political welfare of the millions is paramount to all other questions, and we think that an *annual premium*, given by the National Association for the best plan or essay in furtherance of that great object, would call forth much valuable information on the subject.

While proposing these various means for the political and social amelioration of the people, let it not for a moment be supposed that we agree with those " educationists" who consider the working classes " *too ignorant for the franchise.*" So far from giving countenance to such unjust and liberty-destroying notions, we think the most effectual means to *enlighten* and *improve* them is to place them on a footing of political equality with other classes. We have seen one contracted scheme of improvement after another prove abortive; and we feel certain that theory on theory will continue to be promulgated in vain, till the millions can be interested to carry them into effective operation. 'But what faith can the people have in the professions of men who, while they talk of *instructing* them, are devising and executing the most infamous of laws for restricting the freedom of opinion, the right of public meeting, and the free circulation of knowledge? How can they expect any portion of intelligent workmen to join in any plan of education which excludes one of the most important branches of knowledge—a knowledge of their political rights and obligations? and how can this be taught to and appreciated by men, *without the possession of the rights and privileges of freemen?* How can they trust the sincerity of those persons who would mould them into more tractable and ingenious machines for the production of wealth, but would deny them any political power to determine how that wealth should be distributed? And how can they who make a profession of liberality suppose the working classes are so blind and ignorant as not to see through their speciousness and hypocrisy, when their speeches, votes, and conduct on all questions affecting the rights and interests of labour, prove them either staunch supporters of the present oppressive and fraudulent system, or humanity-mongers, who would make the millions *comfortable slaves*, ignorant of the rights and privileges of freemen, and content at all times to obey the desires of their political and spiritual masters?

Those men who talk of the franchise of the millions as a *boon*, and insist on its being given for particular talents or conduct, seem to forget that in doing so they assume the position of *despots;* nor can they defend it by any other argument than the usual one of despots—*that of force.* For it stands as evident to reason as the existence of the sun, that all "NATURAL RIGHTS" must justly appertain *to all in common.* That as the injustice and force of tyrants led men to congregate in society to protect themselves against aggression, and to secure their natural rights by CONVENTIONAL ARRANGEMENTS, every man in society must stand upon a footing of perfect equality, to determine the nature and extent of those arrangements. In other words, *all men are politically equal* to decide what the *Constitution* of their country shall be, and what *laws* shall be enacted to carry that Constitution into effect. And whatever power stands opposed to this just principle being carried into operation is *a despotic power;* worse in character, if possible, than the first savage tyrants who interfered with the natural rights of their fellows, and first caused them to have recourse to conventional security. For men in their primitive state stand on nearly an equality to contend with their fellows for the subsistence nature affords them; but in *an unjust state of society* despots plunder and murder *in the name of the laws*, and bribe one part of the community to keep the other part in subjection. It forms no argument against this clear principle *of political equality*, to say that the origin of society is involved in mystery—that principles cannot be recognized in old countries which might suit a new colony or infant state of society—that this being a conquered country, the terms prescribed by the conqueror and his descendants led to a state of political thraldom from which we are being gradually emancipated. To all this we reply, that neither antiquity, custom, nor force can be made to usurp and supersede human rights, *without a violation of justice*. We are therefore justified in designating as *despots* all those who, *under any plea whatever*, withhold or oppose our political rights, and in maintaining that they cannot defend their conduct upon any principles of justice. By usurpation and injustice have the few obtained power and ascendancy, and fraud and force are their only title-deeds; and it would be far more honest for them to assume the frank and open daring of other despots, than to be continually cheating us with unmeaning sounds of freedom. Let men and things be properly designated: England with all her professions is but a *despotism*, and her industrious millions *slaves*. For men possessing the same natural capabilities, cast upon the same kindred spot, with the same wants and mutual obligations, *who are constrained by the mandates and force of their fellows* to labour to support them in idleness and extravagance, are *social slaves ;* and all who oppose their emancipation from such a state are *political despots*.

But while we contend that the *suffrage* should not be dependent on any amount of education, we are far from being satisfied with the education or knowledge possessed by the working classes, or, indeed, by any other class in society. The rich and the middle classes are *said* to be better educated than the poorer classes ; but if by " education" is understood the just developement of all the faculties, to the end that men may be *morally* as well as intellectually endowed, we think *the fruits* of that great superiority would be more strikingly exhibited than they are. If, for instance, our titled and wealthy aristocracy were " properly educated," we should perceive its effects in a diminution of their luxury and extravagance—in their abhorrence of war, duelling, seduction, and adultery—in their renunciation of gambling, demoralizing sports, and brutal pastimes—in their giving up the dishonourable practices of bribery and political corruption—in their anxiety to abolish the game laws, corn laws, poor laws, and all the cruel and atrocious enactments they have called into existence for their own exclusive and selfish purposes ; and, in lieu thereof, we should see them devoting a large portion of their extensive revenues to such works and means as are best calculated to *upraise* the toiling millions, and employing the power and talents they possess in promoting knowledge and happiness at home, peace and civilization throughout the world. If our clergy received "*a proper education*," they would be more disposed to practise the precepts of their "lowly master"—they would think less of splendid endowments, and more of their toiling curates—they would abjure fox-hunting, gluttony, and excess—they would leave tithes to their rightful owners, and would honestly and fearlessly denounce "the oppressor, and him who grindeth the faces of the poor." If our commercial, manufacturing, and middle classes of society were "*well educated*," they would abjure the fraud and gambling transactions of the stock-exchange; there would be less commercial swindling—less lying, cheating, and over-reaching in trade; and bankruptcies and insolvencies would be seldom heard of. And if our own brethren were *properly educated*, the despots and tyrants of the earth would soon become rational members of society, *for want of tools to work with;* but as long as they can engage knaves and fools to carry their dishonest purposes into execution, they will continue to maintain their pernicious authority over all the rest of society. If men were *morally* educated, they would shrink with abhorrence from the mercenary occupation of a soldier, and spurn the livery and brutal instruments of his profession. They would greatly question the *honour* of being enlisted in a service in which they would be compelled to fight against liberty abroad and the rights of their brethren at home. The *thirst for glory*, by which despots and tyrants induce their ignorant and brutal slaves to rush like blood-hounds to the slaughter of their fellow-men, carrying rapine, famine, and desolation in their train, would, if men were morally instructed, be properly designated *a thirst for blood*. Glory and honour would change their character with the enlightenment of opinion. While the trade of human butchery would be execrated, men would win the glory and approbation of their fellows by just deeds and benevolent actions; and him whose exertions were *the most useful* would be esteemed as *the most honourable*. Nor would true courage be wanting when necessity required it; for while intellectual men, in possession of their rights, would always be inspired with bravery to defend them, they would scorn to be used as instruments of aggression or defenders of injustice. If our countrymen were *properly instructed*, all attempts to establish *a new standing army of policemen* would have been fruitless. They would have inquired *the necessity* for those blue-coated auxiliaries of oppression—this new amalgamation of watch, spy, and bludgeon-men—this new concentration of force in the hands of an exclusively-elected and irresponsible power; and finding them *intended to check the advancement of liberty*, and perpetuate the reign of wrong, they would indignantly refuse to become such degrading instruments of injustice, and the fingers of scorn and derision would be pointed against their badge, livery, and calling.

Were all men *educated* in a knowledge of their *rights* and *duties*, we should not find any so base as *to sell their votes* for money, place, or influence; nor so self-degraded as to fight *the election battles* of the aristocracy for a modicum of drink. Those who would buy their seats to sell their country would find an empty market; their "open houses" would be opened in vain, their false professions would be disregarded, their threats and intimidations would be treated with contempt. Men politically wise would be strong in principle and united in justice against all such *conspirators* against their liberties. They would weigh against each proffered bribe the political and social evils it would be certain to entail on themselves and their neighbours, and all selfish considerations would yield to conscientious duty. They would carefully scrutinize the professions and principles of their candidates, and would prefer political honesty to shining talents. They would consider their representatives as worthy *servants*, to be rewarded for their irksome duties; and not political *masters*, to scorn and oppress those they have purchased.

If men, too, were generally imbued with that *independent feeling* which springs from the cultivation of intellect, they would never permit their children to wear the badge and livery of *charity*. Wealth and pride might then devise their ridiculous dresses, their foolish decorations, and servile rules in vain; men would have more regard for their children than to suffer them to be exposed to the taunts and ridicule of their fellows, and would fear that the feelings of inferiority and dependence which the circumstances of a charity-school engender in the youthful mind would tend to destroy the independent spirit and dignity of manhood. Though poverty might prevent them from educating their children to the extent of their wishes, they would never allow it to plead an excuse for their degradation; but love and duty would prompt them to employ their leisure hours in instructing their families, or they would abridge their own necessaries to pay others for doing it.

While we rejoice at the progress of knowledge and the improvement that is being effected among our brethren, we cannot fail to perceive the obstacles to their liberty and impediments to their happiness which ignorance still presents, and the glorious change which a wise system of education would produce. Were men mentally and morally educated, most of those *social dissensions* which now mar the peace and happiness of society would cease to exist. That contentious, jealous, and undermining spirit, which is still too prevalent amongst them, would give place to unity, honesty, and plain dealing ; and an interchange of kind feelings and benevolent actions would serve to lighten their toil, and cheer their hours of leisure. Intellectual men, too, would regard their *homes* and their *families* with far different sensations than are felt by those superficial and thoughtless members of society who seek for pleasure and gratification anywhere rather than at home ; by which conduct habits of dissipation are generated on the one hand, carelessness and bickerings on the other ; and domestic happiness, being thus undermined, tends to the destruction of their peace and the ruin of their families. Rightly constituted minds, on the contrary, would feel that, of all other pleasures, *those that spring from domestic happiness are the most enduring and substantial.* Esteeming their wives as *their equal companions*, and not the mere slaves of their passions, they would labour to cultivate their mental powers, to the end that they should participate in their views and feelings, and be the better prepared to train up their children in knowledge, virtue, and the love of freedom.

A deep conviction, therefore, of the necessity of some practical scheme of education being adopted for the working and middle classes in particular, has induced us to submit for their consideration the plan described, so that whilst they are labouring to obtain " the Charter" they shall be instructing themselves, so as to realize all its advantages when obtained ; and not for them to be engaged, as reformers have heretofore, in periodically arousing the public mind to the highest state of excitement, suddenly to sink into apathy *with* or *without* the attainment of their object, as their unity of action, strength or sternness of purpose, may chance to have been exhibited. Those fits of political excitement, however necessary under existing circumstances, betoken an unhealthy state of public feeling; for were men generally acquainted with their rights and duties, they would be ever on the watch *to prevent* political evils, and be continually *perfecting* their laws and institutions, coolly, deliberately, and determinedly. Sound views and just principles, as soon as promulgated, would be caught up, and the resolution to carry them into practice would be recorded with their votes, and expressed by a unity of sentiment and action no government could resist. But while we would urge on our brethren to contend for the principles of the PEOPLE'S CHARTER, and think the plan of the NATIONAL ASSOCIATION the best means to effect it, we feel satisfied that they will still have to acquire the knowledge and cultivate the feelings we have described, before they can enjoy the full fruits and blessings of freedom. Let us remember that the *power* each individual may possess to effect good of any description is of little value, unless the necessity for effecting it is made evident to his understanding, and his feelings sufficiently interested to prompt him to action; and as society is a congregation of individuals, the *political power* they may possess to promote their social or political welfare will be alike fruitless, unless they possess the knowledge and virtuous disposition to use it to the public advantage. Hence it must be evident to every reflecting observer, that *true liberty* cannot be conferred by acts of parliament or decrees of princes, but must spring up with public enlightenment and public virtue. The *power* of the people may subdue tyranny, remove corruption, and establish just and free institutions, but the fruits of their victory and noble purposes will principally depend on the amount of the public patriotism and private virtue which exists among them.

In the plan of the NATIONAL ASSOCIATION, we have provided for the admission of *female* members on the same conditions as *males;* and as some prejudices exist on the subject of female education, and especially against their obtaining any knowledge of politics, it may be necessary to give a few reasons in support of our proposition. As regards politics, *the law does not exempt women from punishment any more than men*, should they trespass on the rights or injure the person or property of their neighbour; and therefore, by all *just* constitutional arrangements, *all should share in the enactment of laws to which they are amenable.* If a woman be a *householder*, she must contribute her share of *direct taxes:* and if not, on all her eating, drinking, and wearing, she contributes her portion of *indirect taxes* equally with men: and according to the unperverted spirit of our Constitution, *there should be no taxation without representation.* Again, if a woman is married, *her influence, for good or evil,* is still exercised in all the political affairs of her husband; and if *single,* her political knowledge or ignorant prejudices are equally powerful in society. Therefore, their rights and influence being manifest, the necessity for *their political instruction* must be equally obvious. But, what is still far more important, women are *the chief instructors of our children,* whose *virtues* or *vices* will depend more on the education given them by their mothers than on that of any other teacher we can employ to instruct them. If a mother is deficient in knowledge and depraved in morals, the effects will be seen in all her domestic arrangements; and her prejudices, habits, and conduct will make the most lasting impression on her children, and often render nugatory all the efforts of the schoolmaster. If, on the contrary, she is so well informed as to appreciate and second his exertions, and strives to fix in the minds of her children habits of cleanliness, order, refinement of conduct, and purity of morals, the results will be evident in her wise and well-regulated household. But if, in addition to these qualities, she be richly stored with intellectual and moral treasures, and makes it her chief delight to impart them to her offspring, they will, by their lives and conduct, reflect her intelligence and virtues throughout society; for there has seldom been a great or noble character who had not a wise or virtuous mother. Our first ideas are received from a mother's eye, and much of our temper and disposition depend on the characters we trace there; her kindness and benevolence give us peace and joy, but her angry frowns and capricious temper terrify us, and injure our whole infantile system. As our perceptions are awakened and faculties matured, her wise or foolish conduct towards us leaves lasting impressions of good or evil; her habits, conversation, and example are readily imitated, and form the foundation of our future character. Seeing, then, that so much of our early education depends on the mental and moral qualities of women, should we not labour, by every means in our power, to qualify them for these important duties? And when, in addition to these considerations, we take into account *how much of men's happiness depends upon the minds and dispositions of women*—how much of comfort, cheerfulness, and affection their intelligence can spread in the most humble home—how many cares their prudence can prevent, and their sympathy and kindness alleviate, it ought to redouble our anxiety to promote the education and contend for *the social and political rights of women*.

While treating of the advantages to be derived from the establishment of district halls, we have, in a great measure, confined our observations to the improvement of adults; and now we think it essential to point out to our brethren the importance, necessity, and advantages of properly educating our children, the faculties such places would afford for that purpose, and to add our meed of information as to the best means of effecting it.

ON THE IMPORTANCE OF GENERAL EDUCATION, AND THE MODES TO BE PURSUED IN THE DIFFERENT SCHOOLS.

In endeavouring to point out the social and political importance of education, and the necessity for establishing a *better* and more *general* system than has hitherto been adopted in this country, it will be advisable to begin by giving a clear definition of what we mean by the term "*education*."

As it applies to *children*, we understand it to imply *all those means* which are used to develope the various faculties of mind and body, and so to train them, that the child shall become a healthy, intelligent, moral, and useful member of society.

But in its more extended sense, as it applies *to men and*

nations, it means all those varied circumstances that exercise their influence on human beings from the cradle to the grave. Hence a man's parental or scholastic training, his trade or occupation, his social companions, his pleasures and pursuits, his religion, the institutions, laws, and government of his country, all operate in various ways to train or educate his physical, mental, and moral powers; and as all these influences are perfect or defective in character, so will he be *well* or *badly educated*. Differences of character will be found in the same class, according to the modified circumstances that have operated on each individual; but the *general character* of each class, community, or nation stands prominently forward, affording a forcible illustration of the effects of individual, social, and political *education*. According to *the mental or moral instruction each* INDIVIDUAL *may receive*, will he be the better able to withstand social taint and political corruption, and will, by his laudable example and energy, be advancing the welfare of society, while he is promoting his own. According *to the intellectual and moral spirit which pervades* SOCIETY, will its individual members be improved; and in proportion as it is ignorant or demoralized, will they be deteriorated by its contact: and *as despotism or freedom prevail in a* NATION, will its subjects be imbued with feelings of liberty, or be drilled into passive slaves.

Our present object is with INDIVIDUAL EDUCATION, beginning with *childhood;* and if we can so far succeed as to interest and induce others to assist in promoting this department of education, the social and political education we have referred to will be comparatively an easy task;—for if the rising generation can be properly educated, in a few years they will give such a healthy tone to society, and such an improving spirit to government, that old prejudices, vices, and corruptions, must speedily give way before them.

We have said, that education means the developing and training of all the *faculties* of mind and body. By *the faculties of the body* we mean the whole physical structure. By *the faculties of the mind* we mean those powers we possess for perceiving, acquiring, and treasuring up various kinds of knowledge; for using that knowledge in comparing and judging of the properties of things, and weighing the consequences of actions; for giving us a love of justice, rectitude, and truth; for prompting us to acts of benevolence, and delighting us with the happiness of others ; for appreciating the beauties of earth and heaven, and inspiring with wonderment, awe, and veneration : in short, all those mental powers which perceive, reflect, and prompt us to action.

By training or educating a *bodily faculty* is meant the means used for accelerating its growth, and adding to its strength and activity. For instance, a proper quantity of nutritious food, pure air, warm clothing, and sufficient exercise are necessary to the proper developement or growth of a child; and if these essentials are denied him in infancy, he will be stunted in growth, and debilitated bodily and mentally; nor can any subsequent treatment effectually remedy the evil. Nay, not only in infancy, but at every period of our existence, are these conditions necessary to health and strength. We might here adduce a great number of facts, to prove the great *physical* injury sustained by infants and adults among the poorer classes from bad or scanty food, impure atmospheres, over exertion, and the evils attendant on ignorance and poverty; but let one or two suffice. M. Villermé, an eminent statician of France, has proved that there are one *hundred* deaths in a *poor* arrondissment while there are only *fifty* in a *rich* one; that, taking the whole population of France, the rich live *twelve and half years longer than the poor ;* that the children of the rich have the probability of living *forty-two years and half,* while the children of the poor have only the probability of living *thirty years.* And the late Mr. Sadler has shown that as many persons die in *manufacturing districts* before their *twentieth* year, as in agricultural districts before their *fortieth.* These alarming facts should awaken the attention of the working classes in particular, and should lead them to investigate the more immediate *cause* of this lamentable sacrifice of life, and to devise some means by which the evil may be remedied.

But we have talked of *training* as well as developing the physical faculties. What we mean by *training a faculty* is this : we mean the subjecting it to a course of discipline, so as to strengthen and habituate it to perform certain operations *with ease and effect.* Thus the muscles of the body may be enlarged and strengthened by *proper* training; the hand may be trained to peculiar performances; the eye to perceive the nicest distinctions of art, and the ear, of various sounds. Indeed, there is this wonderful peculiarity in our organization, *which points out to us our duty*, in the *proper* use and exercise of every part of the mind and body, that the vital current may flow in that direction, not only to repair the waste consequent on that exercise, but to enlarge and strengthen it to perform its operations with greater ease; and the reverse of this is manifest when any part of the body or mind is not exercised or disciplined, as it then loses its energy and power of performance.

We have said that the mental powers have *various* and *distinct* properties; and though it is not necessary to our object to go into the particulars of these, nor the various metaphysical opinions respecting them, it will greatly assist us in our explanations, to describe them as *intellectual* and *moral faculties;*—all of which faculties may be *well* or *badly trained*, according to the knowledge and discipline bestowed; in other words, as the indvidual may have been subjected to a PROPER or IMPROPER COURSE OF EDUCATION.

A man's *intellectual faculties* may be highly cultivated, and yet he may be a very worthless and immoral member of society, for want of that *moral education* necessary to control his animal feelings, and to direct his intellect to the performance of his social and political duties.

Another man may have his *moral faculties* disciplined to perform continuous acts of kindness and benevolence, and may possess the strongest feelings of awe and veneration; and yet, for the want of *intellectual cultivation*, may have his goodness of disposition daily imposed upon by knaves and impostors, and his credulity diverted to superstition and fanaticism.

The *animal faculties* being in common with the brute creation, he who is without *intellect* to guide and *morality* to direct them, will differ little from the brutes in the gratification of them.

Examples of great *intellectual* attainments *without morality* are to be found among all classes of society; from the university-taught gentleman who uses his talent to gratify his interest or ambition *at the expense of justice,* to the experienced swindler or learned impostor, who lives by defrauding and imposing on his fellow-men. And no men are fitter or more likely to become the *dupes* of such persons than those whose *moral* faculties are matured and *intellectual ones neglected*. Examples of strong *animal propensities*, without the reins of intellect and morality to govern them, are seen in those mothers who spoil their children by their ignorant indulgence of their inclinations; in those unions founded *on mere animal love* or instinctive attachment, which occasion much social misery; in gluttony, drunkenness, profligacy, debauchery, and extreme vice of every description. Hence it will be seen that "EDUCATION," to be useful, such as will tend to make wise and worthy members of the community, must comprise *the judicious developement and training of* ALL *the human faculties*, and not, as is generally supposed, the mere teaching of "*reading, writing, and arithmetic,*" or even the superior attainments of our colleges, "*Greek, Latin,* and *polite literature.*"

We have said that good education embraces the cultivation of *all* the mental and bodily faculties; for be it remembered, *that all individuals* (unless they are malformed or diseased) possess the same kind of faculties, though they may materially differ in size and power, just as men and women differ in size and strength from each other. All men are not gifted with great strength of body or powers of intellect, but all are so wisely and wonderfully endowed, that all have capacities for becoming intelligent, moral, and happy members of society; and if they are not, it is *for want of their capacities being so properly cultivated*, as to cause them to live in accordance with the physical laws of their nature, the social institutions of man, and the moral laws of God. Education will cause every latent seed of the mind to germinate and spring up into useful life, which otherwise might have lain buried in ignorance, and died in the corruptions of its own nature; thousands of our countrymen, endowed with all the capabilities for becoming the *guides* and *lights* of society, from want of this glorious blessing, are doomed to grovel in vice and ignorance, to pine in obscurity and want. Give to a man knowledge, and you give him a light to perceive and enjoy beauty, variety, surpassing ingenuity, and majestic grandeur which his mental darkness previously concealed from him—enrich his mind and strengthen his understanding, and you give him powers to render all art and nature subservient to his purposes—call forth his moral excellence in union with his intellect, and he will apply every power of thought and force of action to enlighten ignorance, alleviate misfortune, remove misery, and banish vice; and, as far as his abilities permit, to prepare a highway to the world's happiness.

There is every reason, however, for supposing that many persons have been led to doubt the great benefits of education, from what they have witnessed of the dissipated and improper conduct of those who have had great wealth expended on their education; and that others, observing the jealousies, contentions, and ambition of men *professedly* learned, have been led to inquire " whether *educated men* are happier than those who are *ignorant*." But from want of moral training in unison with intellectual acquirements, such characters cannot be said to be " educated," in the proper sense of the term; they have knowledge without wisdom, and power without the motive to goodness. But as regards " *happiness*," (which may be defined to mean the highest degree of pleasurable sensations,) we think we may safely aver that *the ignorant man can never be truly happy*. He cannot even enjoy the same *animal* happiness in eating, drinking, and sleeping as the brute; for the demands society requires from him in return for these enjoyments give him anxieties, cares, and toil which the brute does not experience. The instinct, too, which nature has bestowed on the lower animals to guide their appetites, seems to give them superior advantages over a man destitute of knowledge. For, ignorant of his own nature, and needing the control of reason, he is continually marring his own happiness by his follies or his vices. Wanting *moral perceptions*, the temptations that surround him frequently seduce him to evil, and the penalties society inflict on him *punish him without reclamation*. Ignorant of the phenomena of nature, he becomes credulous, superstitious, and bigoted—an easy prey to the cunning and deceitful; and, bewildered by the phantoms of his own ignorant imaginings, he is miserable while living, and afraid of dying.

But, it may be asked, what proofs can be adduced to show that *the truly educated man is the happier for being so?* We will anticipate such a question, and endeavour to afford such proofs as, to us, appear clear and conclusive. In the first place, nature has given to most of her children a *faculty* for acquiring knowledge, which, once *quickened and directed by education*, is continually gratified with its acquisitions, and ever deriving fresh pleasures in new pursuits and accumulation of knowledge. To give the greatest delight to those who wisely exercise this faculty, nature has provided a multitudinous variety to be investigated and enjoyed; she has spread out her wonders around them, and unfolded her beauties to their gaze. By giving them the power to transmit their acquirements to posterity, she has opened to their mental view the whole arcana of science and range of art, to afford them unlimited sources of enjoyment.—In the next place, nature has in her bounty conferred on them all the *powers* of moral superiority and social gratification, which, if *wisely cultivated*, afford them pleasures inexhaustable. Those noble attributes of man's nature, ever stimulating him to great deeds and good actions, cast a continual sunshine over the mind of him who obeys their dictates; they render his life useful, and give him peace and hope in the hour of death. Nor can any *cultivated man* for a moment doubt these positions; he has the proof and evidence in his own feelings, and his righteous actions will afford the best testimony to the rest of mankind.

From what we have said on the *nature* and *intention of education*, we think its importance must begin to be evident; for what man is there who, in inquiring into the laws of his nature, finds that his own *individual happiness* is a condition dependent on the cultivation of his mental and moral powers, but will readily admit the importance and necessity of *proper education?*

But let us proceed from *individual* to *social* considerations, (for individual happiness seems to be dependent on social arrangements,) and inquire *how far a man's happiness is marred or retarded by the ignorance, and the consequent vices, that prevail in society.* If his acquirements enable him to perceive the necessity for improving the social institutions of his country, in order to advance the prosperity, knowledge, and happiness of his neighbours, *their* prejudices, selfishness, and cupidity are formidable obstacles to deter him from the attempt. If he be engaged in any trade or profession, and desire to exercise his calling with honesty and conscientiousness, he is exposed to the united rivalry of all those who find their gains promoted, and rank upheld by dishonesty and injustice, or the fraudulent system they have established is such as speedily to drive him from his business or consign him to poverty. If he be the father of a family, and desirous of promoting the happiness of his children by rendering them intelligent, moral, and useful, he cannot with all his anxiety guard them from the contaminating effects of social vice. The ears of his children are assailed by brutal and disgusting language in the midst of his dwelling, their eyes meet with corruption and evil in every street, and seductions and temptations await them in every corner. Should their youthful years be happily preserved from those influences, they are no sooner ushered into *society*, than they are beset with all its selfish, lying, defrauding, and mind-debasing vices; and they must be strong indeed in mind and steadfast in morality, to withstand these tests without pollution;—and many a fond parent who has reared up his children with tender solicitude, whose most cherished hopes have been centred in their welfare, has seen them all gradually engulphed in the vices and corruptions of social life. If a man be poor, he is subjected to all the evils of social injustice; and if he be wealthy, his life and possessions are continually jeopardised by the vicious and criminal victims of ignorance: in fact, in no situation in society can a man be so circumstanced, as to escape the evils inflicted or occasioned by the ignorance of others.

Can any man of reflection fail in perceiving that most of these social evils have their origin in ignorance? *What but the want of information to perceive their true interest, and the want of moral motives to pursue it*, can induce the *wealthier* classes of society to perpetuate a system of oppression and injustice which in its reaction fills our gaols with criminals, our land with paupers, and our streets with prostitution and intemperance? What but the want of intellectual and moral culture occasion our *middle-class population* to spend their careworn lives in pursuing *wealth* or *rank* through all the soul-debasing avenues of *wrong;* and, after all their anxiety to secure the objects of their ambition, find they have neglected *the substantial realities of happiness* in the pursuit of its phantom? And what shall we say of that large portion of our population who have been born in evil and trained in vice?—nay, whose very organization, in many instances, has been physically and mentally injured by the criminality of their parents?* Their perceptions continually directed to evil, their notions of right and wrong perverted by pernicious example, and thereby taught that the gratification of their animal appetites is the end and object of their existence, can we wonder that they become the hardened pests of society, or, rather, the *victims of social and political neglect*—beings whom punishments fail to deter from evil, and for whom prisons, penitentiaries, laws, precepts, and sermons are made in vain? What man, then, perceiving these lamentable results of ignorance, and possessing the least spark of benevolence, is not prepared at once to admit the necessity for beginning our social reformation *at the root of the evil*, by establishing a wise and just system of education?

But if we want further proofs to convince us of its necessity, let us turn from our *social* to our *political* arrangements. The fact of an insignificant portion of the people arrogating to themselves the political rights and powers of the whole, and persisting in making and enforcing such laws as are favourable to their own " order," and inimical to the interests of the many, afford a strong argument in proof of the ignorance of those who submit to such injustice. And when we find that vast numbers of those who are thus excluded readily consent to be drilled and disciplined, and used as instruments to keep all the rest in subjection, the proofs of *their* ignorance appear conclusive. And even those who possess the franchise, (or nominal power of the state,) if we may judge from their actions, are not more distinguished for their wisdom than those mercenaries; for, after selecting their representatives in the most whimsical manner—some for their titles of nobility or honour; others for their lands, interest, or party; and some for having *bought them* with money or promises—they support them in every extravagance and folly, and submit to be plundered and oppressed in a thousand forms, to uphold what they pompously designate " the *dignity* of this great nation." And surely the annual catalogue of crimes in this country of itself affords lamentable proofs

* For cases of idiotcy, lunacy, and mental and bodily weakness, arising from the drunken and dissipated habits of parents, see Mr. Esquirol, Combe, and others, on mental derangement.

of the ignorance or wickedness *of public men,* and their great neglect of their public duties. Those will stand in the records of the past as black memorials against the boasted civilization and enlightened philanthropy of England, whose legislators are famed for devising modes of punishing, and in numerous instances for fostering crime, exhibiting, year after year, presumptive proofs in their omission to prevent it. It will be said of them, that they allowed the children of misery to be instructed in vice, and for minor delinquencies subjected them to severity of punishment which matured and hardened them in crime; that, callous to consequences, they had gone through all the gradations of wretchedness, from the common prison to the murderer's cell, that their judges gravely doomed them to die, gave them wholesome advice and the hopes of repentance; and, when the fruits of their neglect and folly were exhibited on the gallows, they gave the public an opportunity of feasting their brutal appetites with the quivering pangs of maddened and injured humanity. Whether, then, we view man individually, socially, or politically—whether as parent, husband, or brother, there is no situation he can be placed in, in which his happiness will not be marred by ignorance, and in which it would not be promoted by the spread of knowledge and wisdom.

Convinced of the *importance* of an improved system of education, we think there needs little to convince any one of the necessity of its being made as *general* as possible ; for, if the effects of ignorance are so generally detrimental to happiness, the remedy must be sought for in the general dissemination of knowledge ;—we see and feel enough of the effects of partial knowledge, to warn us against the evil of instructing one portion of society, and suffering the other to remain in ignorance. What, but the superior cunning and ingenuity of the few, and the ignorance of the many, have led to the establishment of our landed monopoly in its present state—our trading and commercial monopolies—our legislative and municipal monopolies—our church and college monopolies—and, in short, all the extremes of wealth and wretchedness which characterize our fraudulent system ? In fact, the cunning and trickery which uphold this system have become so evident, that all those who seek to profit by it, are not so much induced to send their children to schools and universities to acquire knowledge for its own sake, or to make them *better* or more *useful* members of society, as they are to qualify them *to rise in it;* in other words, to enable them to live in idleness and extravagance on the industry of other people. This state-pauperizing disposition, this aristocratic contempt for all useful labour, is to be traced to our defective education; and knowledge will be found to be the only remedy for this, as well as for the vices, follies, and extravagances of the few. If the blessings of education were generally diffused—if honesty and justice were daily inculcated among all classes of society, it would, ere long, lead to a more just and general diffusion of the blessings of industry. But as long as one part of the community feel it to be their interest to cultivate mere *power-and-wealth-acquiring knowledge*, and, as far as they can, to prevent or retard the enlightenment of all but themselves, so long will despotism, inequality, and injustice, flourish among the few; and poverty, vice, and crime, be the lot of the many.

But, while we are anxious to see a *general* system of education adopted, we have considerable doubts of the propriety of yielding such an important duty as the education of our children to any government, and the strongest abhorrence of giving any such power to *an irresponsible one*. While we are desirous of seeing *a uniform and just* system of education established, *we must guard against the influence of irresponsible power and public corruption;* and, therefore, we are opposed *to all concentration of power beyond that which is absolutely necessary to make and execute the laws;* for, independent of its liability to become corrupt, it destroys local energies, and prevents experiments and improvements, which it is most desirable should be fostered, for the advancement of knowledge, and prostrates the whole nation before one uniform, and, it may be, despotic power. We perceive the results of this concentration of irresponsible power and uniformity of system lamentably exemplified in Prussia, and other parts of the continent, where the lynx-eyed satellites of power carefully watch over the first indications of intelligence, to turn it to their advantage, and to crush in embryo the buddings of freedom; and, judging from the disposition our own government evince to adopt the *liberty-crushing policy* of their continental neighbours, we have every reason to fear that, were they once entrusted with the education of our children, they would pursue the same course to mould them to their purpose. Those who seek to establish in England the continental schemes of instruction, tell us of the intelligence, the good behaviour, and politeness of their working-class population; but they forget to tell us that, to talk of right or justice, in many of those countries—to read a liberal newspaper or book, inculcating principles of liberty, is to incur the penalty of banishment or the dungeon. They forget to tell us that, with all the instruction of the people, they submit to the worst principles of despotism; that life and property, as well as all the powers and offices of the state, are mostly vested in one man or his minions, and that the vilest system of espionage is everywhere established to secure his domination. They omit to inform us, that parents are compelled, under heavy penalties, to send their children to the public schools, where the blessings of despotism, and reverence for the reigning despot, are inculcated and enforced by all the arts and ingenuity submissive teachers can invent; and that all those who brave the penalties, and teach their children themselves, are subject to infamous surveillance, and their children declared incapacitated to hold any office in the state. Bowed down and oppressed as we already are, we manage to keep alive the principles and spirit of liberty; but, if ever knavery and hypocrisy succeed in establishing this centralizing, state-moulding, knowledge-*forcing* scheme in England, so assuredly will the people degenerate into passive submission to injustice, and their spirit sink into the pestilential calm of despotism.

With every respectful feeling towards those philanthropists whose eloquence first awakened us to the importance of education, and whose zeal to advance it will ever live in our remembrance, we have seen sufficient to convince us that many of those who stand in the list of education-promoters, are but state-tricksters, seeking to make it an instrument of party or faction. We perceive that one is for moulding the infant mind upon the principles of church and state, another is for basing its morals on their own sectarianism, and another is for an harmonious amalgamation of both; in fact, the great principles of human nature, social morality, and political justice, are disregarded, in the desire of promoting their own selfish views and party interests. From the experiments already made, at home and abroad, they see sufficient to convince them of the importance of early impressions; and hence their eager desire to mould the plastic mind to their own notions of propriety. They also see that the flood-gates of knowledge are opened, and that its purifying stream is rolling onward with rapidity; and fearing their own corrupt interests may be endangered, they seek to turn it from its course by every means and stratagem their ingenuity can invent.

If our government were based upon *Universal Suffrage* to-morrow, we should be equally opposed to the giving it any such powers in education, as some persons propose to invest it; its power should be of an *assisting* and not an *enforcing* character. Public education ought to be *a right*—a right derivable from society itself, as society implies *a union for mutual benefit*, and, consequently, *to provide publicly for the security and proper training of all its members.* The public should also endeavour *to instruct the country*, through a board of instructors, (popularly chosen,) on *the best plans of education or modes of training;* and should induce, by prizes or otherwise, men of genius and intelligence to aid them in devising the best. After their plans have been matured, and the greatest publicity given to them, the people should be called upon to choose (by universal suffrage,) two members from each county, to form a special body, *to consider such plans*, and to amend, adopt, or reject them, as they may think proper; leaving those in the *minority* to adopt such plans as their constituents may approve of, till the merits of the plans selected by the majority became obvious to all. Such a mode as this would be more in accordance with liberty and justice than the legal enforcement of any particular plans of education, as of all other subjects it involves greater consequences of good or evil. Government, then, should provide the means for erecting schools of every description, wherever they may be deemed necessary; and empower the inhabitants of the respective districts to elect their own superintendents and teachers, (if. qualified in normal schools,) and to raise *a district rate* for the support of the school and remuneration of the teachers. If we had a liberal government to do this for education—*if the whole people were to be interested in the subject, through popu-*

lar election, instead of a select clique, we might safely trust to the progress of knowledge and power of truth to render it popular, as well as to cause the best plans, ere long, to be universally adopted. But from our government no such liberality is to be expected—we have every thing to fear from it, but nothing to hope for; hence, we have addressed ourselves to you, working men of Britain, and you of the middle classes who feel yourselves identified with them, as you are the most interested in the establishment of a wise and just system of education. And we think we have said sufficient to convince you of the necessity of guarding against those *state* and *party* schemes some persons are intent on establishing, as well as to induce you to commence the great work of education yourselves, *on the most liberal and just plan you can devise*, and by every exertion to render it *as general* as possible; hoping that the day is not distant *when your political franchise will give you the power to extend it with rapidity throughout the whole empire.*

Having briefly given our views of the nature, intention, and importance of education, the next part of our subject necessarily embraces *the particular description of education to be pursued in the different schools*, and *the best mode of imparting it.*

The first difficulty we shall have to surmount in our progress will be *the teaching of the teachers;* and the particular instruction, or mode of training, which they will require, necessarily appertain to the NORMAL OR TEACHERS' SCHOOLS. The establishment of one (at least,) of those schools should therefore be one of the first objects of the association. Whatever may be its particular plan, we think it should be so constructed as to contain an infant, preparatory, and high school, into which children of all ages should be admitted, and in which the persons learning to be teachers shall be taught a *practical* knowledge of the system of education. It should also contain a library, museum, laboratory, sitting-rooms, and sleeping-rooms for the teachers and directors. There should be two general teachers, or DIRECTORS, possessing an intimate knowledge of the best plans and modes of education, and well qualified in the art of imparting it with effect and kindness of disposition. While every encouragement should be given for the *gratuitous* instruction of all those desirous of being qualified as *teachers*, great care and discrimination would be necessary in guarding against the admission of persons who possess neither the disposition, aptitude, nor capabilities for efficient teachers. The educational students should commence with the infant school, and, when proficient in that department, should proceed to the preparatory school; and so on, till they become conversant with every part of the system.* Their time should be so divided, that it should be spent in the schools, and in studying the best works on the subject; in attending to the lectures or discourses of the directors, and in discussions and conversations among themselves. The *time* necessary properly to *qualify a teacher* must (in our first arrangements,) be made to depend on the judgment of the directors; but after our plans are matured, it may be found necessary to fix the time each person shall study in a normal school to qualify him or her for a teacher; and eventually no persons should be employed in the schools of the association but those who could produce *a certificate*, signed by the directors, testifying their competency. But one important duty must not be neglected by the people themselves— *that of rewarding and honouring the teachers of their children*, as this will be the best means of perfecting the science of education, by an accession of men of genius and intelligence, who otherwise will seek rewards and honours in other pursuits.

THE INFANT SCHOOL.

A school of this description might be conducted by a female teacher and an assistant, if the teacher had received her instruction in a normal school. The first requisite she should possess, is a disposition to win the affectionate confidence of the little beings committed to her care ; to effect which, she must supply the place of an attentive, kind, and intelligent parent. *The first object to be achieved, is to render the school-room a little world of love, of lively and interesting enjoyments;* and its attainment will mainly depend upon the benevolent, cheerful, and instructive disposition of the teacher.

* While the male teachers should pass through all the schools in rotation, the female teachers might be limited to the *infant* department of education.

Her acquirements should extend, in the first, to *a general knowledge* of the human frame and constitution, and *the best mode of preserving the children in* full health and vigour, embraced in the terms PHYSICAL EDUCATION.

Second, she should have *a clear idea of the human intellect*, and should possess a *knowledge* and *aptitude* for judiciously developing its perceptive, comparative, and reflective powers, comprised in the words INTELLECTUAL EDUCATION.

Third, she should fully comprehend *the moral capabilities*, and *the laws which govern the feelings;* and should understand *the means by which they may be so quickened, directed, and trained*, that the child shall aspire to greatness and goodness of character, and be able to govern his passions by his reason;—the whole expressed by the terms MORAL EDUCATION.

In addition to these *essential requisites*, she should possess a knowledge of music, have a voice for singing, and be able to express herself clearly and grammatically. She should also possess the love of order, have a refined taste, should be courteous in her manners, and prudent and respectful in her whole conduct. For as her peculiarities will be readily imitated by the children, and her example produce a lasting effect on them, she should be to them, as far as possible, *a standard of excellence worthy of imitation*.

It has been found by experience that the best mode of establishing an infant school is to begin with a few children ; and, after they have made some little progress, gradually to introduce others. By this means, a system of order will be sooner established than if a great number be brought together at once.

The school hours must necessarily vary in different districts, according to the habits of the people ; but whatever time is fixed on for the opening of the school should be punctually observed. The boys and girls should enter by their respective doorways, and each one, being provided with a place in the *cloak-room* for his or her hat or cloak, should be instructed to hang it under a particular number ; they should then proceed to their seats in the school-room, which should have corresponding numbers. As a means of cleanliness and health, door-mats should be placed at each entrance, and cleanly habits in every particular must be scrupulously insisted upon. Some little trouble will be necessary at first to enforce those two essentials, cleanliness and punctuality of attendance; but by judicious management, in a short time the public opinion of the school will extend to the homes of the children, and serve to awaken inattentive parents to their duties. At the ringing of a bell, the school should be formally opened by the children singing some appropriate piece, and no person should be admitted into the room until its conclusion. They should then be engaged with their lessons in the school-room, and amusement and exercise in the play-ground, alternately, according to the state of the weather, and the arrangements of the school; but one great point to be attended to by the teacher, is not to allow them to be over-exerted either with their lessons or their play, though the air, exercise, and *moral training* of the play-ground are of paramount importance.

The classification of both sexes, according to their ages, will be found necessary, as there is reason to suppose that the older children will be more advanced in knowledge than the younger, and because they are too apt to tyrannize over them. They should therefore be *classed*, six or eight in a class, as may be found most convenient; and a class-teacher should be appointed weekly to each class. This method of causing children to teach each other is so much in accordance with their desires and feelings, begetting in one an anxiety to qualify himself to teach, and calling forth the mental and speaking faculties of the other, that this of itself is sufficient to cause us to revere the name of Joseph Lancaster. The *class-teacher* should see to the attendance, cleanliness, order, and proficiency of his class; and should be carefully watched, to see that he properly and courteously perform his duties. He should, however, have no power in the play-ground;—when there, he should have full and unconstrained liberty, as the other children, subject only to the watchful eyes of the teacher and assistant.

Having slightly glanced at these preliminaries, we now come to the mode of education; and here we would especially impress on you, that *no faculty of mind or body can be educated without it is properly exercised.*

In *physical education*, for instance, the mere teaching of a child that pure air and exercise are necessary to preserve him in health and strength, is of little use; he must not only be made to perceive, by a judicious course of instruction, *how* and *why* they are essential, but he must be made *to feel their importance*, by such *proper means of exercise* as the play-ground should afford, till the conviction and habit became blended, as it were, with his very nature. He should be made to understand, by the most simple explanations, why *pure air* is necessary to health, and how all kinds of animals linger and perish if they are deprived of it. He should have the different parts of the body familiarly explained to him, and a general idea given of his animal functions; and *why it is* that *exercise* is necessary to health and strength. There will be some difficulty in conveying this knowledge to a child; but unless a general idea of it be conveyed, the mere *advice* or *precept* to do or avoid doing any particular act will be useless. He may be constrained to perform any duty in obedience to the commands of his parents or his teachers, just as a dog is taught to fetch or carry a stick; but *the importance of doing it* will have no effect, till they are fixed by conviction and rooted by habit. If, however, the teacher fully understands these subjects herself, and has an aptitude for conveying knowledge, she will, by a little additional trouble, make them clear to her pupils; and in her subsequent teaching she will find herself well rewarded for having laid a good foundation.*

The best description of exercise is *that which brings the greatest number of muscles into proper exertion, and which, at the same time, affords rational pleasure.* Much, however, remains to be done in devising proper exercises for children;—many of those in common practice are found to produce physical injury to weak constitutions, and others to produce irrational associations. The *rotary swing*, which is used in many schools, is well adapted for strong children; *shuttle-cock*, if played with both hands—*dancing* in the open air— together with such evolutions as may describe the actions

* For the most clear and detailed information regarding the structure and functions of human beings, we would refer the reader to "The Philosophy of Health," by Dr. Southwood Smith; to "The Principles of Physiology," by Mr. A. Combe; to "Dr. Hodgkin's Lectures;" Dr. Brigham on the "Influence of Mental Cultivation and Excitement on Health;" and Mr. G. Combe on the "Constitution of Man."

and habits of different animals which children are fond of imitating, will be sufficient exercise for the children in the play-ground. The *manual exercise*, as it is called, descriptive of different notions and actions, will be found highly beneficial for in-door exercise in bad weather. But a skilful teacher will readily invent games and amusements for the children, will join with them in their play, and, when all their faculties are in full activity, will inculcate many intellectual and moral lessons.

In *intellectual education* no *real* knowledge can be acquired but by *the exercise* of the perceptive, comparative, and reflective powers. The child may be burthened with a multitude of words—mere barren symbols of realities of which it has no cognizance, with imaginary notions of every description—mere treasured phrases, imbibed from every scource, without inquiry or knowledge of the reality, —it may be furnished with rules, figures, facts, and problems by rote without examination, and consequently valueless for practical purposes;—all these acquisitions failing to produce *clear ideas*, and forming no *real basis* for reflection or judgment, cannot, therefore, be properly designated *real knowledge*. Yet this word-teaching, rote-learning, memory-loading system is still dignified with the name of " education ;" and those who are stored with the most lumber are frequently esteemed the greatest " scholars." Seeing this, need we wonder that many scholars have so little practical or useful knowledge, are superficial in reasoning, defective in judgment, and wanting in their moral duties ? or that the greatest blockheads at school often make brighter men than those whose intellects have been injured by much cramming ?

Real knowledge must be conveyed by *realities ;* the thing itself must be made evident to one or more of the senses, to convey a knowledge of its form, size, colour, weight, texture, or other qualities. Those perceptive powers, being continually *exercised* by the observation of various objects, become gradually *strengthened* and *matured*, and the knowledge of their qualities rooted in the memory. It is the high cultivation of those faculties that gives the artist and sculptor such nice perceptions of the tints, forms, and symmetry of their productions. In order, therefore, to *educate* the *perceptive powers* of the child, he must be directed to observe things, their qualities must be made evident to his *senses ;* he must be taught, in the first place, to observe their *most obvious* properties and characteristics, and as his mind expands he must be made acquainted with all their other qualities.

After his perceptive powers have been awakened by observation, and the qualities of things impressed upon his memory, the next object is to stimulate and educate his *comparative powers.* To effect which, his attention should be directed to the differences and similitudes of objects in all their various qualities, to compare their relative forms, position, distances, arrangement, number, &c.

Then his *reflective powers* should be directed to the *why* and *wherefore* of all those forms, qualities, analogies, and differences which have previously occupied his attention. This mode of proceeding will gradually cultivate his discriminating and reflective powers as regards *realities*, and will lay the foundation of clear and consecutive reasoning.

But in conveying this knowledge of things to a child, the teacher must be careful as regards over exerting its attention, and also guard against confusing it, which she will be apt to do, if she proceeds to describe or direct attention to one object after another in rapid succession, and goes through all their various qualities, uses, &c. She must proceed step by step, and be certain that her little pupils have clear ideas on one point before she proceeds to another; otherwise they will get confused, or *imbibe her explanations by rote, without understanding them.* The teacher should also see that, while the children's attention is directed to the acquisition of the various kinds of knowledge referred to, they should be taught the *medium* by which they acquire it; that is, they should be familiarly and practically taught the uses of the *senses.*

But in teaching children a knowledge of *things*, a knowledge of *words* must not be neglected; and in the usual mode of teaching those two essentials, there appears to us to be a deficiency for which we presume to suggest a remedy. The deficiency seems to us to be in this particular: the child's attention is first directed to things and their qualities, and the *words* which express them are repeated by the teacher; and according to the strength of the child's memory they are retained there. His attention is next directed to a *reading* lesson, (probably with a picture at its head;) now, though he may have pre-

viously heard the various *words* of this lesson, or may
have many of them treasured up, yet, when he sees
them in print, they appear to him as Greek or He-
brew characters appear to us, and he has to undergo a *second* discipline, to enable him *to connect the
ideas he has retained in his memory with those words;*
or, if he has not retained the ideas previously taught him,
he has to get the words by rote. In short, there appears
to be wanting in this mode of teaching *a closer connection of words and things.* The following plan for their
more intimate connection will, in our opinion, effect this
object ; and will also supply the best *spelling* and *reading
lessons* for the INFANT SCHOOL, and in the PREPARATORY
SCHOOL will be found highly useful for teaching a knowledge of *grammar* and *composition.*

*A Case of Moveable Types.**

ABCDEFGHIJKLMN	
OPQRSTUVWXYZ&.	
BCDEFGHIJKLMN	A Pea.
O QRSTUVWXYZ&.	
a b c d e f g h i j k l m n	
o p q r s t u v w x y z &.	Tin is heavy.
b c d f g h i j l m n	
o p q r s t u v w x y z &.	
t t t o o o i i i a a a e e e	Wax is soft.
s s s r r n n u u h h h d d.	

The above sketch represents a case, or shallow box,
containing moveable types or letters, constructed as follows : The types should be made of beech, about a quarter of an inch in thickness, and varying in size according
to the size of the letters. The letters should be *printed*
in large, bold type, on tough paper, and should be fixed
on to the types, (or bits of wood,) with thin glue. Instead of glueing them on singly, it will be better to glue

* Since this was written we have read, in Dr. Biber's Life of
Pestalozzi, that he had in his school *spelling tablets*, in which the
letters were made to slide;—how far our suggestion may be similar
we are not competent to determine, having never seen the invention of
M. Pestalozzi.

them on a slip the whole width of the case, and cut them off with a fine saw, and trim them when the whole is dry. There should be two sets of Roman, and two sets of small capitals, in each case, together with two or three extra of those sorts of letters most used, such as e, t, o, i, a, n, &c. The cases may vary in size as the lessons may require; those twelve inches by ten will be a good size for the infant school. They should be made of plane-tree, or of wood not liable to warp; the sides to be half an inch thick and one inch deep, which should be grooved in the inside for both top and bottom. They should be mitred, keyed, and glued, and the bottom be put in at the same time they are glued together; and slips glued on the bottom in the inside, about a quarter of an inch wide, to separate each row of letters. The types must be made to fit in the case, so that they may easily be picked up; and if the slips between each row are made a little thinner than the types, it will facilitate this. The top, or lid, of the case should be made to slide easily towards the right hand. A number of slips must also be glued upon the lid of the case, (as seen in the sketch,) in which the words are to be *composed*.

We will now endeavour to describe the mode of using those types in the infant school. Instead of "lesson posts," usually adopted in those schools, we would suggest that *stands* (something like a reading-stand) be substituted in different parts of the room, for holding the letter cases; and if they were made with a drawer in each, for containing the *case* and *objects* when not in use, it would save the teacher much trouble. When the time for their *object-lesson* has arrived, the class-teacher marches his little class up to the stand, and arranges them in a half circle; and having properly placed his *case*, and got ready his *objects*, he takes up his position on the right of the stand within the circle, mounted on a little stool, and provided with a short pointing-stick. He then takes an object from his collection, (or shows them the card or picture, as it may be,) and passes it round for the inspection of his class, and then asks them its name. Some one of the children will most probably inform him; but if they are all unacquainted with it, it becomes the duty of the class-teacher to instruct them. Supposing one of them says, " It is a pea," the class-teacher then requests one of them to *compose* " A Pea;" he accordingly picks up the letters from the case, and arranges them (as is seen in the sketch) on its lid.   After it is thus composed, he requests another child to *spell* and *read* what is composed; and so he proceeds, giving them different objects, asking them their names, then to compose those names, and then to spell and read them.   By permitting *those that can* to name the object, will quicken the faculties of all; and by calling upon them *alternately*, one to compose, and another to spell, it will arrest the attention of the whole; when, if they were asked in rotation, those who had had their turn would be inattentive.   In giving this example, however, it is assumed that the children have been previously instructed in a knowledge of the letter case, and also to distinguish the capitals from the smaller letters, and their use.   For the first class of children it will be necessary to select those objects that are easily spelled, as pea, tin, nut, wax, lead, iron, &c.; and, if they are pictures of animals, such as cat, dog, ass, goat, sheep, horse, &c.

After they have thus learned to understand the *words* conveying the *names* of those objects which are easily spelt, their attention should be directed to their most obvious *qualities*, as " Tin is heavy," " Wax is soft," &c., which sentences they should be taught to compose and spell as before.   By thus presenting familiar objects to their senses, then teaching them their names, then the letters that compose them, and then their sounds, we give them *a clear conception of words;* and by their handling the objects and letters, we interest them in every step of their progress.   By this simple contrivance the children can be taught to spell *without the use of books,* and without the mischievous system usually pursued of *tasking* and over-burthening the memory with *words,* which, when acquired, are useless till the objects or qualities they represent are made evident to the senses of the child.   *Reading* can also be taught with facility by this method; and being always in connection *with things and their properties*, the knowledge thus conveyed is more likely to be comprehended and impressed on the memory, than if the child had to spell and stumble his way through a long paragraph, the sense of which he would in all probability lose, from the difficulties he would meet with, and the want of clear and definite associations.   The *ar-*

rangement of the words by the method suggested would also enable the teacher to convey incidentally the *grammatical* meaning of several of them; but this would be of little importance in the infant school. If figures be substituted for letters on the types, the children may be taught *the use and value of figures*, though the *properties* and *elements of numbers* should always be taught by *real objects*; therefore, it would be well to use Mr. Wilderspin's arithmeticon in connection with the types.*　In fact, the *letter-case*, in the hands of a skilful teacher, will, as we conceive, be found a pleasing instrument for conveying a vast fund of information to the mind of a child.

During the time the children are thus occupied with their lessons under their respective class-teachers, the teacher and assistant should be engaged in superintending and instructing them; and a variety of questions may be put and information given at those times, which may have a very beneficial tendency.

In order to impress particular objects on the memory, as well as to cultivate their tastes and perceptions of beauty, the room should be ornamented with well-executed, coloured prints, or drawings, in natural history, zoology, astronomy, and machinery, together with neat models, and a few specimens of minerals and fossils; and at different times their attention should be directed to them, and their use and characteristics explained. The teacher should also give them an idea of angles, squares, circles, &c., from objects, or from various instruments and models, which can be cheaply obtained for that purpose. For instructing them in a knowledge of weights and measures, it would be well if some of the smaller ones were introduced into a corner of the play-ground, as well as some clean sand for the children to weigh and measure, and let them *prove by experiment* that so many ounces make a pound, or pints a gallon; they should,

---

* The *arithmeticon*, invented by Mr. Wilderspin, for the purpose of teaching children the elements of numbers, is an oblong, open frame, with twelve wires running across it at equal parallel distances, on each of which wires there are twelve wooden balls strung, making in all one hundred and forty-four. The balls are the size of a nutmeg, and are painted alternately black and white, which, when used, are passed from left to right, and the children taught to count and understand the numbers.

however, be provided with a scoop, to prevent them from soiling their hands. The most advanced class should be provided with small slates, on which they should be taught to form the outlines of squares, angles, circles, and eventually of letters, by copying from diagram-boards placed slantingly before them on the floor. Nor should their *tuneful* powers be neglected, as the exercise of them would be both healthful and instructive; but care should be taken against practising them in any nursery nonsense, or in compositions they cannot understand. Pieces inculcating their social and moral duties, or descriptive of beauty and perfection in nature or art, will be found the most useful. The children should also be taught *the elements of dancing*, both for exercise of body and cheerfulness of mind. While, however, much *intellectual* knowledge may be conveyed in a pleasing manner to little children, care must be taken *to convey it clearly*, however slowly the progress may be, and also that the child is not forced beyond its natural powers.

Having given our opinion regarding the means of exercising and educating the physical and intellectual powers of the child, it is now necessary to advert to the most important feature in infant training, that of *moral education.* And here we would again premise that *the moral faculties must be positively exercised*, the same as the intellectual or bodily faculties, in order to train or educate them; that is, each faculty must be separately appealed to by some exciting cause, and by constant *exercise and discipline* directed to such course and conduct as shall best promote the happiness of the individual, and of the society of which he is a member.

We have already said that every individual possesses, in common with other animals, a great variety of *animal inclinations;* these are more active in some than in others, but they are more active in all than the nobler faculties, designated *moral faculties.* Those *animal* propensities confer a great amount of happiness on the individual *when they are governed by morality and directed by intellect;* but otherwise, they dispose him to gratify his inclinations selfishly, cruelly, unjustly, and intemperately. On the contrary, it is the nature of the *moral faculties* to predispose him to a love of justice, truth, benevolence, firmness, and respect for whatever is great and good;—*but they need cultivation;* and, unfortunately for mankind, the circum-

stances calculated for their developement and cultivation
are not placed so easily within the reach of individuals as
are those circumstances which develope and bring the *animal* propensities into activity. Perceiving this, the question
for inquiry is, what are the means to be adopted for educating those nobler faculties of our nature, so that in conjunction with knowledge they may be made to direct wisely and
temperately govern the selfish and sensual desires? But will
mere *advice* or *precept* be sufficient for this purpose? will
these be sufficient to educate the *moral* any more than the
intellectual powers of the mind? And what course do we
adopt to cultivate the intellectual faculties of our children?
Are we content with merely *advising* them to read, write,
and cypher? with *lauding the great advantages* of mensuration? or with *promising to reward them*, if they will
but excel in a knowledge of geometry? Certainly not;
for what possible good would such conduct effect? what
conceptions can they form of those various kinds of knowledge, till they are made evident to their senses, and till
their understandings are gradually trained to perceive and
appreciate their importance?—then, indeed, will our *precepts* be responded to by their convictions, but till then
will be of little use. Should not this common sense mode
of educating one set of faculties be our guide for another?
nay, does not experience prove that, if we would succeed
in cultivating the moral faculties, we must proceed in precisely the same manner as we do with the intellectual?
For instance, if we would cultivate *the love of justice* in a
child, we must first make *the idea* of justice evident to his
sense, by pointing out to him such instances of injustice and
impropriety as may occur in his own conduct or in that of
others, and give him the reasons *how* and *why* he should
have acted the reverse. *The love of truth* should be
cultivated in the same manner, though it forms an
almost inherent principle in children, till they are taught
falsehood by the example of their parents or others;
but when so corrupted, they can only be cured by
the same intellectual and moral discipline. *Benevolence, kindness,* and *humanity* must be equally rendered
obvious *to the understanding;* unhappily, examples of
misery, unkindness, and cruelty are everywhere too prevalent. Not that children should be taken out of their
own sphere to witness them, but in their own little circle
every opportunity should be embraced of directing their

attention to any object, incident, act, or anecdote, calculated *to give them correct ideas of the moral qualities
sought to be conveyed*, and then to quicken and discipline
their *moral faculties*.* As one means of calling forth and
educating some of the higher faculties, we would suggest
the establishment of a *sick fund* in every school. By instructing them to make their own rules and conduct their
own business, they will be readily brought to understand
principles of law and justice, and rules of duty and obli-
gation as members and officers; and by their visiting of
their sick members (unless in infectious cases), they may
be practically disciplined in kindness and humanity. It
would be also advisable to instruct them to make or amend
such rules or regulations as may be necessary for the government of their play-ground, which should be hung up
and appealed to when any one offended against them.† All
this may appear to some of trifling importance; but by such
trifles a skilful teacher would convey more practical lessons
of *rights* and *duties* than could be effected by volumes of
theoretical learning. The *right of property* is another important lesson which, if made evident to the intellect, will,
in connection with their love of justice, be found the best
security against all kinds of pilfering and dishonesty. To
call forth their *respect and admiration for all that is truly
great and good*, the teacher should be assiduous in directing their attention to any such acts whenever they occur,
and she should occasionally read and explain to them
anecdotes of great deeds and good actions; not of heroes
and conquerors, the pests of our race, but of those whose
acts and deeds have augmented the amount of human
happiness. They should also be taught the importance of
useful labour and the *value of industry*, by showing them
how labour is required for the cultivation of the earth, in
order to provide us with food, raiment, and habitation, as
well as to convert its productions into articles for our necessity and comfort; and also that our bodies are so organized that the exercise of moderate labour improves our
health;—and, therefore, seeing that labour is necessary, and
that *all* are benefitted by it, *all ought to labour and be*

---

* See a very excellent work by Mr. A. Combe, "On the Management of Infancy," on this particular point.

† The trial by jury, as adopted by Mr. Wilderspin, will be found another important means of moral discipline.

industrious, according to their abilities ; and that all those who, under any pretence, evade their fair share, act unjustly and dishonestly towards their brethren, by imposing on them such additional burthens of labour as to injure their health and diminish their happiness. While they should be taught to value and respect *the acquisitions of honest industry*, they should be made to perceive the injustice of ill-acquired possessions, and to despise every description of luxury, extravagance, and dissipation which corrupts society, and diminishes the general amount of human enjoyment.

Nor must their *imaginative powers* be neglected; to develope which, their attention should be directed to the various points of beauty, grandeur, and sublimity which are seen in the glowing landscape, the flowing stream, the storm, the sunshine, and the fragile flower; and, above all, the radiant glory of a star-light night. Such lessons will teach them to soar beyond the grovelling pursuits of vice and sordid meanness.

As affording the best means of regulating their *appetites and desires*, they should be familiarly instructed in their uses and functions, and shown how undue gratification proves injurious to health and morals;—how *all their faculties of mind and body are governed by peculiar laws*, which laws must be *obeyed*, to insure health and happiness; and that, whenever they are *disobeyed*, sickness of body, pain of mind, or injury to their neighbours, are certain to be the inevitable result.

While much moral instruction may be conveyed in the school-room, the play-ground will be found the best place for *moral training ;* where all their faculties will be active, and when their dispositions and feelings will be displayed in a different manner than when they are in the school-room, where silence, order, and discipline should prevail. But when in the play-ground, the teacher should incite them to amusement and activity, in order to develope their characters; and whenever any irregularity of conduct transpires, she should put forth her *reasons* rather than her authority;—her object should be to *convince*, rather than to chide them. For if she attempts to restrain the passions or govern the moral feelings by a system of *coercion*, she will as surely fail in her object as most of those who have gone before her. Another mental faculty which requires great care and attention is *the love of ap-*

probation ;—this, when properly disciplined, is an essential requisite to greatness of character; but, when otherwise, it degenerates into low and selfish ambition. The teacher would therefore do well *to avoid all kinds of rewards and distinctions,* so as to prevent all kinds of mental rivalry among her pupils; and she should also be careful in her praises and scrupulous in her censures. For though such stimulants may call forth some of their intellectual powers, it will be in most cases at the expense of morality; for while those possessed of strong distinctive feelings will strive to excel and rival their fellows, their triumphs will call forth the envy, hatred, and hypocrisy of all those who are outrivalled. They should all be impressed *with a high sense of duty,* each to perform and excel according to his abilities; and taught that nature having given them all different powers of mind and body, he who cultivates his powers and employs them to promote *the happiness of society* is sure to meet with the approval of all good men, independently of his own conscientious satisfaction. In short, the teacher must make it an especial part of her duty to cultivate *all the moral faculties,* as they are of paramount importance; at least, she must lay a sound foundation. She must remember that each faculty has particular functions to perform, and must be trained according to its peculiarities—that, *necessary to all moral instruction, the intellect must be made to fully understand moral qualities, by rendering them obvious to the senses*—and that each faculty must be awakened and disciplined by constantly *exercising it,* according to its nature, and under the guide of the intellect.

In concluding these general observations on infant training, we have thought it unnecessary to refer to many points of management—to the heating and ventilating of the school, the particulars of the play-ground, or the different kinds of apparatus required for teaching. There is one point, however, necessary to mention, as it involves a proposed alteration—it is this: in most infant schools, they have a *gallery* in one end of the room, for the simultaneous teaching of the children, an arrangement which, we think, might be dispensed with, seeing that the room would be wanted for other purposes of an evening. We would therefore suggest that the side seats (constructed, like steps, one above another, like those generally used in infant schools) *be made moveable,* and *in short lengths,* so that they may be removed of an evening, if necessary; and also, when any simultaneous teaching is required, those at the furthest end of the room may be readily brought up, and extended across wherever they may be needed, so that, when the teacher is mounted on the *rostrum*, the children would both hear and see as well as in a gallery.

THE PREPARATORY SCHOOL.

As will be seen by the plan of the district halls, we propose that the upper room of each be fitted up for the purposes of a PREPARATORY and HIGH SCHOOL, for both males and females, until more extensive arrangements can be made for building a greater number of schools in each district; but in order to preserve the separation of the two schools, as well as that of the two sexes, we recommend the arrangements as seen at page 42, by which it is proposed that the PREPARATORY SCHOOL be situated in the body of the room—the boys on the right hand, and the girls on the left, with a passage between them divided by a moveable hand-rail, or by any other means. And as, in all probability, comparatively fewer children will attend the HIGH SCHOOL, we propose that a division be made in the upper end of the room (as seen in the plate) on each side of the rostrum—the boys on one side, and girls on the other. If, however, the numbers in the respective schools vary considerably, other arrangements can easily be made to accommodate them.

Instead of the usual writing-desks, which cramp the arms and distort the bodies of children, we propose that *tables* be instituted of the height required, made with drawers for holding their slates, books, and school apparatus: and that the *forms* be made with framed backs, as the spine is often injured from long sitting without such support; and if they are made of the height necessary *for adults*, by the placing of a foot-rail in front of the table, they will be equally convenient for the children to sit upon. The *rostrum*, or platform for the teacher, should be made with steps in front, and of a size sufficient for the assistant to sit on; for the lecturers, &c., of an evening. On each side of the room, in the piers between the windows, *stands for the letter cases* should be fixed, and so made, that they may let down close to the wall when not in use.

The school room should be handsomely fitted up and

decorated with maps, drawings, diagrams, and models, illustrative of the various branches of knowledge. There should be a good coloured map of the world, another of Europe, one of the United Kingdom, and, if possible, a *relief* map of the county in which the school is situated. There should also be large prints or drawings of the human skeleton, of the muscular system, and of the interior of the human body; also geological and mineralogical maps of the earth's strata; prints, or drawings of the solar system; of the mechanical powers; of perspective illustration; together with others of a like instructive tendency. It should also be furnished with a pair of globes, with Hadley's quadrant, Fahrenheit's thermometer, the mariners' compass, geometrical models, models for drawing from, a cast or model of the human brain, as well as any curious specimen in nature or art of a useful and ornamental description. The play-ground should also be provided with such useful gymnastic arrangements as may be necessary for the exercise of the children, as well as with any means or contrivance the teacher may think necessary for their instruction. And it would be highly desirable if every such school had a piece of garden attached, by which the children may be taught some practical knowledge of horticulture and botany. They should be allowed at least *half an hour* in the middle of the forenoon and afternoon of each day, as well as their dinner hour, for recreation and amusement in the play-ground, so that their health may be preserved by proper air and exercise, and their youthful spirits kept up in all their buoyancy, which the present system of confinement, tasking, and drilling materially tends to destroy. Any objections that may exist against the association of boys and girls in the same play ground, may easily be obviated by the girls being allowed to play in the ground of the infant school, the time for the infants being there regulated accordingly.

It would be advisable to have no schooling on the afternoons of Wednesday and Saturday, in order that the teacher and assistant might on those times take out the different classes in rotation, to teach them a knowledge of those objects which cannot be properly taught in the school room.

The same order should also be observed in these schools respecting the children's hats, cloaks, and bonnets as in the lower school; a similar system of *classification* should be continued, and the same enforcement of *cleanliness* and *regularity of attendance*.

The schools should be opened of a morning and closed of an evening with *vocal music*, the principles of which should form a part of the children's education; and the teacher should see that they retired to their respective homes with more order and regularity then are generally observed after school hours.

In addition to the qualifications enumerated as essential for the teacher of the INFANT SCHOOL, the teacher in the PREPARATORY and HIGH SCHOOLS should possess the following requisites: he should *write a fair hand*, be a good *arithmetician*, have a general knowledge of *mathematics* and their practical application to the arts of life. He should understand *geography*, so as to explain the position, resources, habits, and pursuits of different nations, and of his own country in particular; he should know so much of *astronomy* as to be able to explain the phenomena of the heavens, and of *geology* and *mineralogy*, as to impart a knowledge of the structure and wonders of the earth; he should possess some knowledge in *natural history*, so as to give an account of the animals on the earth's surface, and especially of his own species; he should have some knowledge of *chemistry* and skill in experiments, and should know so much of *natural philosophy* as to be able to explain the general causes and effects in nature; of *political knowledge* he should understand the basis of rights and duties, the principles and theory of government, the foundation of law and justice, and especially the political system adopted in his own country; he should understand the principles of *political, or national, economy*, comprising a knowledge of the production and distribution of wealth; he should know something of the *philosophy of history*, chronologically and biographically, so as to direct the children to distinguish truth from fable and falsehood, to detect deeds of shame and injustice beneath false coverings of glory and honour, to strip sophistry of its speciousness, interest of its panegyric, and heroes of their hollow fame; and, as far as possible, to extract wisdom from the black record of our species in their advance from barbarism *towards* civilization. He should know something of *botany*, should have a taste for *gardening*, and be acquainted with *agricultural pursuits ;* he should possess a knowledge of *perspective*, and have a taste for *design*, so as to be able to sketch correctly any object of art or nature : in addition to which, it would be well if he understood *the first principles of the most useful trades.*— Many persons may conceive that great difficulties will have to be surmounted before we shall have teachers qualified in all these particulars, and doubtless there will ; but when we take into account the vast number of persons in this country possessing great knowledge and genius, who are now fagging as schoolmasters, clerks, office-writers, authors, or drudges of some kind, *who would readily qualify themselves in a normal school, if by doing so they could improve their condition,* we may safely rely on finding a sufficient number of qualified teachers, if we bestir ourselves to make and extend a profitable market for superior talent.

The teacher's assistant should be able to write well, have some knowledge of arithmetic, should speak grammatically, have some skill in the use of her needle, should understand cutting out male and female garments, should possess a correct taste, have an aptitude for teaching, be of courteous manners, and have a good moral character.

We now come to *the mode of education* to be adopted, and *the particular kinds of knowledge* to be imparted in the preparatory school.

The object of this school being to effect a still further developement of the physical, intellectual, and moral powers, we know *no better mode* than that we have already referred to. To improve the physical powers of the children, the air and exercise of the play-ground will still be necessary; to mature their intellect, their perceptive, comparative, and reflective faculties must be exercised in observing and reasoning on realities; to strengthen and discipline their moral powers, they must be led to perceive and understand *moral qualities,* and be exercised and trained by external impressions.

The *kinds of information* to be imparted, especially to the first class of children, must depend on their previous training; but presuming that they have been strengthened and much improved by going through the discipline of the infant school, we recommend that their attention be now directed to objects and qualities more difficult to comprehend. They should be taught to perceive and understand more minute peculiarities and nicer distinctions, to learn to describe them correctly, to account for their origin and estimate their uses.* Their attention should also be directed to the external world, with all its natural and artificial variety; in *nature* they should be gradually taught to understand the habits, peculiarities, and uses of such animals as they saw, as well as to distinguish the properties of trees and common plants, the qualities of earths, rocks, and minerals, and eventually to distinguish class, genera, order, and species.

In the *artificial* world they should be shown the various descriptions of tools and instruments of labour, and have their uses explained to them; and such kinds of machinery, manual and scientific operations, as they could have access to. In short, their attention should be directed, their inquiries elicited, and their minds informed regarding every object which meets their eyes, or which could be brought within the sphere of their observation.

In order to instruct them still further in the use and meaning of words, as well as the spelling and composing them, THE LETTER CASE should be introduced, and used in a similar manner as in the infant school. Only in proportion as the children advance from one class to another, they should describe the objects presented to them *more at length*, and *correctly compose the different words as they describe them*. After which the class-teacher should turn the letter-case towards him, and request them alternately to *spell* the different words composed, and eventually some of them to *read* the whole composition. While these lessons are proceeding with, the teacher and assistant should see that the different objects are properly described and spelt, that the children pronounce the different words correctly and distinctly, that they read with proper emphasis, and understand the meaning of each word they use.

A great portion of *English grammar* may also be taught through the medium of those compositions, by the teacher instructing the children in the names, uses, and qualities of the different words as they occur. And if the most simple rules in grammar be printed in a large type, hung up against the walls, and referred to, *to guide or correct them whenever it may be necessary*, it will be found that they

---

* The Pestalozzian system of teaching by objects, as set forth in Dr. Mayo's " Object Lessons," would be a great assistance to the teachers.

will be far better understood by such practice, than if they were learned by rote, without any practical means of application. The teacher and his assistant should also direct their particular attention to the *conversation* of the children in the play-ground, and see that they express themselves grammatically, for correct speaking cannot be learned but by continued practice.

We now come to the *writing* department, and here we must suppose that the children have been taught the forms and proportions of letters in the *writing-alphabet* in the infant school; if not, they should be taught in *classes* by the means of diagram-boards placed before them, on which the letters should be drawn, and which the children should copy on their slates. The teacher should direct their attention to the peculiar forms and proportions of the letters, and the easiest method of copying them. As soon as they have acquired some skill in making the letters, they should be taught *to write down the names of objects on their slates*, and a number of objects which are easily spelt should be given to each class for that purpose. After they have had some practice with one set of objects, another should be given them; and eventually they should begin to describe at length their qualities, uses, &c.*

The children should be taught a *small hand:* large hand should never be attempted till they have acquired great freedom in the use of the pen. The absurd practice of *ruling lines* for children should be dispensed with, as it begets a pernicious habit, which makes it difficult for adults so accustomed, to write straight without lines.

The eye must be practised from infancy to direct them to write straightly and evenly, without lines; and though they will write irregularly at first, the advantages will be soon obvious to the teacher.

As they will have to write on slates till they have acquired some proficiency, their pencil should be fixed in a *tin case*, so as to make it the requisite length (about six inches), *which they should be taught to hold as they would a pen.* And in order that it may be always at hand, they should have a small groove made on the top of their slate-

---

* Small boxes (or cards) of objects should be collected and arranged by the teacher for the different purposes of the school; a great variety may be collected in his walks with the children, and others may be purchased at a trifling cost.

frame, of the length required, with a bit of leather over it, in which to keep their pencil.

Nor must the teacher forget to instruct his pupils in *the proper position of sitting to write*, as well as in *the correct movements of the hand, arm, and fingers*, which are essential for writing with elegance and expedition.

The pupil should sit in an upright position near the table, with the left side near, but not pressing it, and with the whole weight of the body supported by the left arm. The body should be bent a little forward, with the right arm resting on the table three or four inches from the body. The slate (or paper when used) should be placed directly in front of the right arm, and parallel with the edge of the table. The pencil (or pen) should be gently held between the thumb and first and second fingers, with the top of it always pointing to the right shoulder. Little children should keep the second finger nearly *half an inch* from the point of the pen, and persons of ten years old and upwards about *an inch*. The fleshy part of the fore arm should rest on the table, so as to give the wrist full play ; the hand may be supported on the ends of the third and fourth fingers inclined towards the palm of the hand.

In *writing*, the letters are executed by *three general movements* and *their combinations*.

The *first movement* is that of the *whole arm* in all directions. To acquire this movement with freedom, the learner should practise exercises in perpendicular columns, where letters or syllables are connected from the top to the bottom by means of loops, which should be executed without taking the pencil from the slate. The movement of the fingers may be *combined* with the arm in these exercises, but the wrist should never touch the table.

The *second movement* is the forward, backward, and oblique play of the *fore arm*, while the arm rests lightly on or near the elbow. The great object in this movement is to discipline the muscles of the fore arm, so necessary to expert and exact penmanship. The learner should, therefore, begin by making ovals either horizontally or obliquely, continuing the pencil on the slate, and going round repeatedly on the same outline as quickly as possible. When the oval can be made with neatness and precision, he should try to make letters and short words, but without lifting the pencil; and the movement of the under fingers must be such that, if another pencil were fixed to them, they would produce the same word at the smae time. In writing current hand by this movement, the learner must slide his arm laterally along the table at convenient distances, so that his hand and elbow be always in a line where the word is to be written, and parallel with the sides of the slate (or paper). The movement of the thumb and fingers is generally *combined* with this movement in all sizes of writing, in free running hand, and in all quick writing.

The *third movement* is that of *the thumb and fingers alone*. Exercises proper to acquire this movement are all common sized large hand, formal small hand, and all studied writing where great exactness is required in the forms of the letters.

As *a general rule*, the pupil should first be taught the use of the arm and fore arm, and till much facility is gained in using them, the use of the fingers in current hand writing should be postponed ; and even when the fingers are allowed, they should not be suffered to execute the whole writing, but only the upward and downward strokes of the letters, while the connecting hair lines are formed by the lateral movement of the arm or fore arm. He should never be permitted to lean on his wrist when writing, nor should his pencil be taken off the slate in the middle of a word.*

By attention to these rules the pupil will be easily taught to write a straight, even, and masterly hand, instead of the stiff, formal, and crooked style so common to those who have been taught by the ordinary methods.

When they can write tolerably well on their slates, they should be provided with *writing-books*, into which they should copy *their compositions on objects*, as well as *descriptions of such places, scenes, or occurrences as they may have witnessed in their walks with the teacher*. It should also be his duty to point out to them particular objects for this purpose, and to question them at the time as regards their several features or peculiarities, in order to call forth *the descriptive powers of the children*:—they should write the matter down first on their slates, and, *when approved of, into their copy-books*. We give the following specimens illustrative of our meaning :—

* The above method of sitting, holding the pen, and movements of the hand and arm, is taken from an article in the Educational Magazine for 1838, edited by Mr. William Martin.

"Last Saturday afternoon our teacher took us to Mr. Carefull's farm, and showed us the tools and implements used in farming. We saw spades, picks, hoes, rakes, pitchforks, scythes, sickles, sieves, and a great variety of other tools, the names of which I have forgotten. We were shown how they used several of them, and had the uses of most of them explained to us. We were then taken to the barn, stable, cowhouse, sheepfold, piggery, poultry-yard, and other places about the farm. We then went out to the fields, and saw the farmer and his men ploughing and harrowing the ground, and sowing wheat. When the teacher informed us of the nature and uses of all those things, I thought that farming was the most useful of all occupations.

"Oct. 24th, 1839.   " RICHARD JONES. "

"The last time I was out with my class we were taken to a blacksmith's shop, where we saw the manner of working in iron and steel. They had a large fire kept up to a great heat by means of an immense pair of bellows ; in which fire they heated the iron, in order to soften it. We saw them make several tools and other articles while we were there. They put the pieces of iron the articles were made with into the fire, and when they were made hot, they took them out with a large pair of tongs, and hammered them into the forms they wanted them, on a large block of iron called an anvil ; they were then filed up very smoothly, and when finished were polished.

"Sept. 11th, 1839."   " JOHN TURNER."

"On Wednesday the 25th of July, 1840, being on the top of Beech Hill, my attention was directed to Widow Neat's cottage, which is pleasantly situated on a rising slope at the foot of the hill. It is but a small and homely built place, yet the taste and industry of Joseph, the widow's only son, have rendered it a little home of beauty. The rough appearance of the walls is concealed by a luxurant vine in front, by a flowering clematis at one end, and a fine peach tree at the other. The garden in front of the cottage is laid out with great neatness, the gravel walks are kept dry and clean, the different beds are edged with box, and I think a more choice collection of blooming flowers and odorous plants are seldom found in so small a spot. There is a small orchard at the back of the cottage well stocked with apple, pear, and plumb trees ; and every part of it is kept in great order. The widow was busily engaged with her needle in a little bower which her son had built for her in one corner of the garden, and her son was industriously employed in the orchard. I was so struck with the neatness of the cottage, the taste and order of the garden, the cheerfulness of the widow, and industry of the son, that on leaving the place I resolved to profit by what I had witnessed.

" WILLIAM JOHNSON."

The children's discrimination and judgment regarding *moral qualities* may be exercised in a similar manner, by teaching them to describe any act of cruelty or injustice, or of kindness or affection, they may have witnessed in their rambles. Their first productions will doubtlessly be very crude, but the mode we have described for calling forth their knowing and reasoning powers, will greatly assist them in composition; and when they know that they will have to describe certain objects they see in their walks, they will observe them with greater care and attention than they otherwise would.

For the purpose of aiding their descriptive and inventive powers, they should also be taught *the art of sketching objects,* as it will be of great service to them in the respective trades and occupations they may hereafter be engaged in. To this end, the sketching classes should first be provided with *geometrical models,* the outlines of which they should be taught to draw by the eye on their slates. After they have had some practice in drawing these symmetrical objects, they should be provided with different sets of *drawing models,* for the purpose of sketching their outlines.* When they have acquired some skill in this branch, they should be provided with leaves of trees and plants to sketch, and eventually with the plants; the wild flowers and weeds they may find in their walks will afford them great variety, and be far better for the purpose than those of the garden. As they progress in the art they should be taught to take sketches of tools, machinery, patterns, buildings, trees, landscapes, &c. They should also be taught the most simple rules in perspective, and also to shade and tint their productions, and be provided with a drawing-book, and encouraged to practise their lessons at home. As accessory to this art, they should be taught to construct the various kinds of angles, ovals, and different-sided figures in geometry, but in all instances familiar applications of them should be brought home to their understanding.

If the children have been trained in the infant school, they will have learned the elements of numbers by means of tangible objects, and they should now be instructed in the use and *application* of the four fundamental rules of arithmetic, simple and compound. And as many children are unfortunately taken away from school before they are nine years of age (the time for admitting them into the high

* These can be cheaply obtained; but if some of the girls were taught "the art of modelling in Bristol board," they could make models of this description.

school), it would be well to teach them in the preparatory school the best and simplest mode of keeping accounts. Among the multiplicity of plans proposed for teaching children a knowledge of arithmetic, the Pestalozzian and the Lancasterian seem to be most generally preferred. The following are brief specimens of each of their plans :—

THE PESTALOZZIAN METHOD.

" The children are taught the *elements* of numbers by *objects*, such as beans, pebbles, small squares of wood, or any other objects at hand.* They first begin by learning to count the objects presented to them. When they are familiar with this, they begin with *addition*, thus : one and one are two, two and one are three, three and two are five, &c., at the same time having objects before them to prove it. They then proceed to *subtraction*, thus: one from five, and four remains ; three from nine, and six remains ; eight from twenty, and twelve remains, &c. Then to *multiplication*, thus : two twos make four, three fours make twelve, nine threes make twenty-seven, &c. Then to *division*, thus : there are three fours in twelve, six threes in eighteen, five eights in forty, nine fives in forty-five, &c. The child is then exercised by means of objects and writing down strokes on his slate, as follows : in six twos how many tens and ones ? in two fives how many tens ? in four threes how many tens and ones ? in nine threes how many tens and ones ? &c. He is then taught the elements of *fractions* by means of small squares of wood, marked on the surface into different squares ; and by them the child is made to perceive that two is the third of six, three the third of nine, five the fourth of twenty, &c. He is then taught by objects the different *powers* of numbers, as thus : the powers of *two* are four, eight, sixteen, thirty-four, &c.; the powers of *three* are nine, twenty-seven, eighty-one, &c. He is thus examined as to proportions : in *three fours* how many ones, twos, threes, and fours are there? in *four fours* how many ones, twos, fours, eights and sixteens are there? &c. After they are well exercised in this manner by means of *objects*, they are exercised in *mental arithmetic ;* that is, they are exercised without the aid of objects. And in order to acquire this kind of knowledge, the same or similar lessons are repeated without objects."

THE LANCASTERIAN METHOD.

" The first class in arithmetic is taught as follows :—The monitor reads from a table, which he is provided with, thus : 9 and 1 are 10, 9 and 2 are 11, &c.; 25 and 1 are 26, 25 and 2 are 27, &c.;—and as he reads, *each child writes it down on his slate.* Other tables are then used for subtraction, as thus : take 9 from 10, and 1 remains ; 8 from 12, and 4 remains. The multiplication and pence tables are taught by the same method. The mode of examining them regarding *what they have learned* is as follows. These tables, *without the totals to them,* are suspended

* Such as the arithmeticon.

against the walls, and the children are arranged in a semi-circle before them. Supposing it to be an *addition* table, the monitor asks the child at the head of the circle how many are 9 and 4;—if he cannot answer him, he asks another child; and so on, till he meets with one who can answer him; and he who answers the question takes precedent and the badge of merit from the child who is unable to answer it. And so the monitors proceed to question them regarding subtraction, multiplication, &c. The next step is to teach them *sums* in the different rules. The monitor, being provided with a written book of sums, begins with addition in the following manner. He reads aloud the first row of figures in the sum, which the children *write down on their slates as he reads them;* and so he proceeds with the other rows, taking care to inspect the children's slates as he proceeds, to see if they have written them down correctly. He then reads from his book the mode of counting up the sum, thus: 7 and 9 are 16, and 3 are 19, and 5 are 24; set down 4 under the 7, and carry 2 to the next. This is also written down by each class as he proceeds. Compound addition is proceeded with in the same manner, as also are all the other simple and compound rules, every rule being a study for a separate class. The mode of examining them regarding what they have learned in these rules is similar to the method above stated. In whatever rule they are in, a sum in that rule is written on a diagram before them, and the children are called on in rotation to work it before their class. Supposing the sum to be in addition, the first boy proceeds to add up *aloud* the first row; if he fails, the next is called on, &c."

A portion of geography should also be taught in this school, not by rote, but, as far as possible, by models, maps, and illustrations. The first essential is to give the children clear ideas of *the general form and surface of the globe*, which, we think, may be brought home to their understandings by the following methods: A *model of the globe* should be prepared, having the portions representing the sea sunk, and those that represent the earth elevated *and made rough*, and both coloured so as to represent land and water. In conjunction with this they should be shown a *relief map of the county they live in,** by which they should be taught to perceive that the rough places on the model are mountains, hills, and valleys, intersected with rivers, lakes, and streams. They should then be taken to the top of some eminence, and shown the surface of the surrounding country, and should be taught to refer to the relief map for the elevations and depressions before them, and to the model of the globe for the roughness

---

* *Relief* maps, published under the patronage of the Central Society of Education, are sold by Taylor and Walton, 28, Upper Gower Street, London.

they perceived on its surface. Having given them clear ideas of the general form of the earth, they should then be taught to understand its most prominent particulars. A continent, island, peninsula, cape, and isthmus, may be illustrated by a small model, in which *water* may be introduced to represent seas, lakes, gulphs, rivers, &c.; and which, in conjunction with the terrestrial globe, will serve to convey clear ideas. They should then be taught to draw the general outline *of their own country*, with its principal rivers, canals, roads, towns, and cities, and to know the staple trade and manufactures carried on at the different places. When thus made acquainted with the geography of their own country, they should proceed in a similar manner with the whole of the United Kingdom.

If they are presented with proper specimens and drawings, and have some attention shown to them in their different composition classes, they will acquire much information in natural history, chemistry, mineralogy, and geology; and in their walks with their teacher, as well as in the garden, they may very easily be taught the elements of botany. The teacher should also devote some portion of time, twice or thrice in the week, for the purpose of giving the whole school *short lectures* or explanations on such subjects as cannot well be conveyed through the means of the different classes, such as the structure and functions of the human body—of the brain, and its functions—the best means of preserving health—the nature of government, laws, rights, and obligations—the production and distribution of wealth—as well as some information and experiments in chemical and mechanical science. But the whole should be conveyed in the most simple and familiar language, and illustrated and explained by such apt comparisons, models, pictures, diagrams, and other means, as a skilful teacher will easily invent and know how to employ.

As a great number of children, either from timidity or the want of a clear perception of the meaning of a passage, fail to read with proper emphasis and effect, we recommend the following mode of practising them in *the art of reading*. A well written and forcible piece should be selected, either in prose or verse, and the teacher should read it aloud, *in conjunction* with two or three classes at once, taking care that each child reads it, word for word, in the same tone and emphasis as the teacher does. By reading all together in this manner, the least variation in tone or emphasis will be easily detected ; and by singling out those who vary from the rest, and drawing their attention to their own faults and the way to avoid them, they will in a short time catch the tone and spirit of the rest, and consequently acquire the teacher's mode and manner of reading.

For the purpose of giving them a taste for reading, and the *power of understanding what they read*, it will be advisable that *lesson cards* be laid before them at stated times, on which some interesting objects should be described or facts narrated, and, after giving them a short time to read and think, *examine them alternately as to the meaning of what they have read.** It will be unnecessary to question them individually; for as they will not know who will be examined, they will all prepare themselves, and consequently all profit by their reading.

In addition to the various kinds of knowledge we have referred to as necessary to be taught *to both sexes* in the preparatory school, it should be the duty of the assistant to teach the girls to knit and sew, to mend and make different kinds of garments, and to impart to them some information on domestic economy.

Kindness and *reason* should always be employed to urge them to their duties, coercion and anger never.

Knowledge should never be made irksome by *tasks* and *compulsion*, but rendered pleasant by means of the clear-headed and light-hearted disposition of the teacher.

THE HIGH SCHOOL.

By the time the pupil has gone through the six years' discipline of the other schools, and arrived at an age to be admitted into the high school, he will not only have acquired much useful information, but will have made great progress in the art of imparting it to others; which is one of the great essentials of education. If proper attention has been shown him, he will possess sound *discriminating* and *reflective powers*—the best guides to knowledge and wisdom; and having been trained in *the practice* as well

---

* See specimens of lesson cards at page 112.

as the knowledge of morality, he will be inclined to pursue truth, justice, and benevolence for their own intrinsic excellence, and conscience giving reward. His memory, instead of being filled with the words and sayings of others, will be stored with a knowledge of things, qualities, facts, events, and conclusions which he has tested by the evidence of his senses, and made his own by his reasoning and experience. His attainments, though as yet little more then elementary, will be varied and extensive, compared with those which are usually possessed by children of his age; and will have been acquired under circumstances of pleasure and amusement, compared with the usual scholastic system. If he has been properly taught, he will have clear ideas of the form and surface of the globe he lives on—will know something of its structure, materials, and inhabitants—as well as the principles and means by which its materials are rendered subservient to the purposes of man. He will have some knowledge of his own nature, bodily and mentally, as also of his rights and duties, his moral and social relations. He will also be familiarised with many important facts and experiments in science—will have clear ideas of numbers and computation—will have made some progress in drawing, and will be able to describe, in a fair hand, and in tolerably correct language, the ideas he has received.

The object of the high school is for the still higher developement of his moral faculties,—to extend his knowledge of arithmetic, geometry, geography, drawing, and composition,—to make him still further acquainted with nature and her laws—with the resources, institutions, and arts of life—with the history of his own species—and to cultivate, as far as possible, his powers of communicating knowledge.

In teaching arithmetic and mental calculation, the clearest and shortest system should be adopted. We have already referred to that of Mr. Wood; the next which appears to us to possess great merits, is Messrs Willcolkes and Fryer's system; the following two or three examples will convey a slight, though a very imperfect idea of their work.*

* Printed by Henry Mozley and Sons, Brook Street, Derby; and sold by Longman and Co., Paternoster Row, London. Price 5s.

What will 36lbs. cost, at 11d. per pound?

	£	s.	d.
36 at 1d is equal to .	0	3	0
Multiplied by .			11

£1 13 0 Ans.

What will 71 gallons cost, at 11s. per gallon?

71 at 1s. is equal to .	3	11	0
Multiplied by .			11

£39 1 0 Ans.

What will 80 yards cost, at 4s. 3d. per yard?

80 at 1s. is equal to .	4	0	0
Multiplied by .			$4\frac{1}{4}$

£17 0 0 Ans.

3d. being the $\frac{1}{4}$ of a 1s., the $\frac{1}{4}$ of £4 is added.

Whenever a *practical* method or application of any rule in arithmetic can be shown, the teacher should always avail himself of that mode of instructing the children; and the same may be said of mensuration, geometry, and trigonometry, which should be taught by the most approved methods, in the last year of their schooling. Their knowledge of perspective should be extended, and their practice of drawing continued in this school; and especially in the art of drawing tools, implements, machinery, plans, &c. They should also be further instructed in the geography of the United Kingdom, and eventually in that of the whole world.

The system of reading from cards should be continued in the lower classes, but the lessons should treat of higher subjects, such as the various phenomena of nature, the properties of different kinds of matter, the structure and functions of the body, the nature of laws, government, &c. And in the higher classes they should commence with history, beginning with that of their own country; and when they are well informed in that, they should proceed to the history of other countries.* We

* See the " History and Resources of the British Empire," the " History of the English Language and Literature," price 2s. each ; the " Histories of Greece and Rome," 2s. 6d. each; and a variety of other excellent school-books, published by William and Robert Chambers,

think that the mode of reading and examining them in *classes*, as suggested in the PREPARATORY SCHOOL, will be found the best. It will be advisable for the teacher to examine them as to the meaning of any particular word in their lessons; each class should be provided with dictionaries to refer to, and to prepare themselves to understand the meaning of what they read.*

To practise them in writing and composition, the system of describing the objects, scenes, and events, they may observe in their walks with the teacher should be continued, and in the school-room, such as the teacher may present to them for that purpose. They should also be instructed as regards force, clearness, and beauty of style, in their compositions; and the higher branches of English grammar.†

If, as we have suggested, they have been taught from infancy to describe the nature and qualities of such things as have been presented to their senses, they will have acquired a great facility of expression, and have much valuable information to impart. The next great object to be achieved, in order to render them useful in proportion to their knowledge, is to practise them in *the art of expressing themselves correctly and coherently*. Most persons possess powers of language which, if properly cultivated, would greatly extend their usefulness in society. We therefore suggest the following method for cultivating the art of oral expression:—The children being classified according to their ages or capacities, one in each class should be selected every day, to give an explanation of some object, or to deliver a short lecture on some subject which the teacher may select for him, before the members of his own class. Every pupil called upon to lecture, should have a day to prepare himself, and should select the subject he is best acquainted with. Suppose he is called upon to explain the nature and use of *copper*, he will proceed to describe its nature in the ore, and in its pure state—its pecu-

Edinburgh; and sold by W. S. Orr, and Co., London; and all book-sellers.

* The "Etymological Dictionary," and "Student's Manual," by R. Harrison Black, LL.D., are works which should be found in every high school.

† See "Parker's Progressive Exercises on English Composition."

liarities, properties, and all he knows respecting its uses; and at the same time exhibit to them such specimens as the museum or laboratory will afford. After he has concluded, in order *to test their knowledge*, the members of the class should be encouraged to question him respecting any point in his discourse. The higher classes might be called upon to give a short account of some matter in history or science, or other subject they may be acquainted with. Their first attempts will doubtlessly be weak and disjointed, but as they proceed they will acquire confidence and facility, and at the same time will be acquiring a great deal of valuable knowledge. Having a day to prepare themselves, they will be able to collect their information and arrange their ideas; and as they will be subject to the examination of their class, under the encouraging eye of the teacher, they will strive to excel both in the delivery and knowledge of their subject.

For the purpose of instructing the higher classes still further in chemical or mechanical science, the teacher would do well to devote a portion of time, one or two evenings in the week, for giving lessons and performing such experiments in the laboratory as would not be healthy nor convenient to perform in the school-room in his ordinary lectures.* And some of the most skilful members of the association might be employed of an evening to instruct the biggest boys in the use and management of tools in the workshop.

The children should also be encouraged by their parents, at home, to make collections of books, drawings, prints, minerals, plants, or anything of an instructive or amusing character; as such pursuits will call forth habits of frugality, taste, order, and refinement, which all the precepts in the universe may fail to effect.

In the industrial and agricultural schools a similar system of education should be adopted *for the orphan children of the association*, excepting that in the AGRICULTURAL SCHOOL a portion of their time should be devoted to the cultivating of the farm, and in the INDUSTRIAL SCHOOL to such manufactures or occupations as

---

* We would especially recommend to the teacher the mode adopted by Mr. Reed for teaching chemistry, &c., by which the children are instructed to perform all the experiments themselves.

may be combined with it. We think that they should continue in these schools till the age of twelve or fourteen, and then that suitable masters should be provided for them.

Such is the general mode of education we would suggest for training up the rising generation in knowledge, morality, and the love of freedom.

In describing the numerous advantages likely to result from forming an association upon the plan suggested, we have deemed it a portion of our duty thus to direct the attention of our working-class brethren, in particular, to the great importance and necessity of education. But in putting forth our views on this branch of the subject in a plain and, as we conceive, a practical form, we do not imagine we have given birth to any new plans or originality of method. Seriously impressed with the evil to be apprehended from any state-moulding system of instruction, conducted by and for the interest of party,—and, moreover, perceiving the great and beneficial advantages likely to result from a just system of education, under the control of the whole people, we have been influenced to devise and promulgate what we conceive to be a means by which the *evil* may be avoided and the *good* gradually achieved. Being in a prison, we have found some difficulty in proceeding as far as we have, for the want of such books and facilities as our liberty would have enabled us to obtain; but, in all probability, if we were in the enjoyment of that inestimable blessing, the pressing demands of our families, and the active pursuits of life, would have so far engaged our attention, as to have prevented us from ever writing anything on the subject. In what we have written we may not have expressed ourselves as correctly and guardedly as the subject merits, but we trust that the liberality of our countrymen will lead them to excuse these defects in persons who have not had the advantages of a literary education, but who are nevertheless desirous of arresting the attention of working-men who, like themselves, are desirous of obtaining better governors, wiser measures, and happier times than the present.

As some *legal* difficulties may be started in objection to the plan proposed, it may be well to anticipate them, and to give our opinions on the subject. In the first place, the existing laws are opposed to the formation of any association which is composed *of separate branches*, each branch having *distinct officers*, and corresponding with each other. But the members of the NATIONAL ASSOCIATION, in whatever part of the country they might reside, would form but *one general association*, having *one general fund*, and governed by *one general set of officers*. Though the GENERAL BOARD is proposed to be elected in different counties, on account of the difficulties that exist of calling any general meeting to elect them, they being elected by *members of one association*, and being appointed to conduct that *one association only*, would be perfectly a legal body. The subsequent appointment of *superintendents*, to manage the district halls when erected, being of an *educational* character, would not be any more amenable to law than are the arrangements of the British and Foreign School Societies. So far we have deemed it necessary to explain our conceptions of the infamous and atrocious laws of Pitt, Castlereagh, and Sidmouth. But, taking into account the important objects contemplated by this plan, that of uniting and inducing the people to erect halls in different parts of the country, for the purpose of instructing themselves and their children to become wiser and better members of the community, any government who would presume to bring forward any tyrannical or obsolete statute to prevent or crush such a righteous measure, would bring down upon them the just indignation of every reflecting mind in the country to scare them from their unholy purpose. But such attempts we neither apprehend nor fear—the object is just, the cause is worthy of sacrifice; and whenever our brethren are disposed to unite hand and heart to endeavour to carry this *or any other better plan into practice*, we shall be found among their number.

SPECIMENS OF LESSON CARDS.

ON TRUTH.

A truly *intellectual man* is distinguished by his earnest desire to know *the truth* of every proposition and opinion presented to his notice; and a truly *moral man*, by his resolves to pursue it at all risks, and *to practise* its dictates regardless of all consequences.

By such united efforts of *intellect* and *moral principle* has the progress of society been effected—have despotic cruelty, fanatic zeal, and superstitious frenzy been moderated; and by the continuation of such potent efforts will truth and justice eventually prevail over error and wrong.

Unhappily, however, truth is slow in its progress; the cause of which is to be traced to the idleness, vanity, bigotry, and interest which prevent the generality of mankind *from examining the opinions they entertain*, as by such culpable neglect old errors are fostered, and new vices transmitted to posterity.

The opinions of men influence their actions; and while such as are founded *on truth* are generally the precursors of good and virtuous actions, opinions which are founded *on error* are mostly the parents of evil. The man, therefore, who honestly investigates the opinions he holds, discharges a great *moral duty* to society; while he who receives without examination and believes without inquiry, is guilty of a *moral offence.*

But if to hold opinions ourselves, without investigating the evidence on which they rest, be so far immoral, how much more so is it to instil such opinions *into others*— which, whether true or false, beneficial or mischievous, *we have never taken the trouble to inquire!*

And yet this is not only daily done among every class and grade of society, but we too often see the influence of *persecution* and the rod of power brought in to enforce their unexamined crudities and presumptuous zeal.

Had such persons been accustomed to examine their own opinions, they would not fail to perceive that *the evidence of truth is irresistible,* and that *reason* is far more efficient than *persecution* to carry conviction to the mind.

In order to arrive at the truth of any opinions we entertain, two essentials are necessary: one is *to "be industrious in collecting all the evidence we can obtain on which our opinions rest;"* and the other, *to "examine it carefully, when collected, without being influenced by interest, party, or prejudice, to incline to the one side more than to the other."*

When a man bestows such pains to arrive at *truth,* he will find his opinions will stand the test of investigation, his intellect will be strengthened, his moral principle invigorated, his means of usefulness increased, and his sympathies extended towards the whole human family.

GEOLOGY.

Whenever we dig through the vegetable or surface soil which covers our globe, we come to other substances; such as clay, sand, pebbles, chalk, and rocks of different descriptions.

The science of geology teaches us that these substances are not promiscuously blended together to form the globe, *but are arranged in layers, one above another, all around it,* like the different coatings which form an onion, though it seldom happens that they are found so regularly disposed.

For though they appear to have been originally deposited in regular horizontal layers, (or *strata,* as they are called by geologists,) the volcanoes, earthquakes, and other convulsions of nature, have since greatly changed their position.

In some places we find these strata so pushed outward as to form *hills,* at other places so sunk inward as to form *valleys,* at others so lifted up and broken that *their ends are seen on the surface;* and sometimes the *lava,* or melted rocks from the volcanoes, has been *forced up through the different strata,* so as to form the highest mountains above them.

These strata are composed of different substances; some of sand, as the sandstone; some of trees and vegetables, as the coal; and some of shells and other marine productions, as the limestone;—these seem to have been *gradually deposited* in the bottom of the seas and lakes which formerly covered the earth, and in the lapse of ages have either been *converted into stone,* or into the substances as we now find them.

The proofs that they are so composed, and have been so deposited, are numerous ; for instance, some of the highest hills are found to be composed of different strata of rocks, in which the remains of fishes, shells, corals, and other marine productions are embedded, which must have been deposited there when the substance which forms the rocks was in a muddy, granular, or fluid state.

If these animal remains, instead of being gradually deposited by the sea, had been washed there by it, we should find them deposited against *the sides of the hills;* and should also find *the heaviest materials at the bottom,* in a confused and mixed state ;—instead of which, we find them in layers running through the body of the hill, and some of the angles of the shells are as well preserved as if they had lived and died on the spot.

Those rocks which have been deposited in layers, or strata, are called *stratified rocks;* and those which have been forced up through them in a melted state, are called *unstratified rocks,* such as granite, whinstone, and basalt.

The stratified rocks are very numerous, and are divided by geologists into three great divisions, called the *transition, secondary,* and *tertiary formations.*

On examining the animal or vegetable remains (or *fossils,* as they are called) contained in these different rocks, they find additional proofs for believing that what is now land was once seas and lakes, and that great changes of climate must have taken place on the surface of the globe.

It is also found that race after race of animals has existed and disappeared from the earth, some of them of gigantic and wonderful forms.   The remains of some that have been found show that they must have been nearly a hundred feet long, and some so large that the socket of the eye measures fourteen inches and half in its diameter.

But among all these fossil remains, *those of human beings are not found,* proving that hundreds of thousands of years must have elapsed, and the earth been occupied with one race of animals after another, before man made his appearance on the surface of the globe.

MINERALOGY, &c.

The science of *mineralogy* teaches the nature and peculiarities of rocks, stones, and metals, though it is sometimes divided into *lithology,* or the study of earths and stones, and *metallurgy*, or the study of mineral substances.

The metals are the heaviest bodies in nature. They melt, and for the most part acquire lustre, by the action of fire: those that are *malleable*, or will spread out under the hammer—and *ductile*, or will bear to be drawn into wire, are the most valuable. There are *forty-two* different kinds of them, the most useful of which are gold, silver, copper, tin, lead, iron, zinc, mercury, bismuth, cobalt, manganese, platinum, and antimony.

Gold, silver, and copper, are occasionally found in a *pure state*, but are more generally found blended with other substances, as are all the other metals. When any metal is found pure, it is said to be in its *native* state, as "native gold or silver;" but otherwise it is called *ore*, as "copper or iron ore."

The metals are generally found in the oldest rocks, such as the *primary formations;* in which are also found the *gems*, or precious stones, such as the diamond, ruby, garnet, topaz, emerald, amethyst, &c.

The metallic ores are found embedded in fissures, or cracks of the rocks, called *lodes;* they vary in length from a few yards to several hundreds, and in width from a few inches to several feet, and sometimes they run to an immense depth;—there is seldom, however, more than one kind of metal in each lode.

There are great difficulties in getting the ore out of these lodes;—first, on account of the hardness of the rock; and second, on account of the springs of water which are mostly found in it.

To get rid of the water, they sink a very deep well, or *shaft*, into which the water is drained, and pumped up by means of the steam-engine.

They force their way down through the rock by boring it, and blowing it up with *gunpowder*, the force of which shivers the rock for some distance, which they then break through by means of their picks, large hammers, and iron wedges. They not only proceed downwards in this manner through the lode, but they work their way through it horizontally. The upright pits are called *shafts*, and the horizontal cavities *adits*.

The *ore* which they find is broken into small pieces, and drawn up in large iron buckets, by means of machinery; after which it goes through different processes, called *dressing*, and eventually is sent to *smelting-fur-naces*, to be purified by fire.

Those *shafts* and arrangements for getting the ore are called *mines;* the persons employed in the works are called *miners;* and the operation is called *mining*.

THE STOMACH.*

When the food is *masticated*, or chewed, it passes into the stomach, to undergo a process called *digestion*.

The stomach is an oval-shaped, muscular bag, with an opening at each end; the one called the *cardiac* orifice, where the food enters—and the other, the *pylorus*, by which the food passes into the body when digested.

It is formed of two strong layers, or fibrous membranes, one above another, and is lined with what is called the *mucous coat*.†

In the outside membrane the fibres run lengthway of the stomach, and in the middle one they run round it, so that, when they contract, they give to the stomach *a worm-like motion*, by which the food is kept in agitation till it is digested.

The lining of the stomach has a velvety appearance, of a pale pink colour; it is gathered up into folds, and wrinkled so as to grasp the food; and, when in a healthy state, is continually secreting a mucous fluid, to soften and keep it in order.

The stomach is also covered with a great number of blood-vessels and nerves, which pass through it in all directions.

In the lining of the stomach there are also a vast number of very minute vessels, which secrete the *gastric*, or stomach juice; which is a transparent fluid, of such a digestible, or solvent nature, as readily to convert all kinds of solid food into *chyme*.‡ The sensation of *hunger* is occasioned by these vessels becoming over filled. When there is no food in the stomach, it is collapsed and inactive; but as soon as food enters it, it begins at once to be

---

* The facts in these *physiological* lessons are principally derived from "The Philosophy of Health," by Dr. Southwood Smith; from "Physiology" and "Dietetics," by Dr. Combe; and from Dr. A. Brigham, on "Mental Cultivation."

† Mucous—*the tongue and nostrils are covered with mucous coats.*

‡ Chyme—a soft, pappy-like state.

excited, the blood rushes towards it with great force, the gastric vessels begin to secrete their juice, *which mixes with the food in eating*, and the muscles of the stomach set it in active motion till digestion is completed. When water or ardent spirits are taken into the stomach, they are not digested, but are immediately *absorbed* by the innumerable small vessels which everywhere cover its surface.

There is only a *limited quantity* of gastric juice secreted—more or less, according to the health of the individual; and if more food is taken than there is juice to mix with, it will lie in the stomach *undigested*, till nature recruits her powers to supply more.

The stomachs of adults will contain about three pints.

THE INTESTINES, LIVER, PANCREAS, AND OTHER DIGESTIVE ORGANS.

When the food is digested in the stomach, and converted into *chyme*, it has to go through other changes, before it enters the blood, and gives nourishment to the body.

As soon as it passes out of the stomach, in the state of chyme, it enters the upper end of the intestines, or bowels, which is called the *duodenum*, from its length being the breadth of twelve fingers.

When in the duodenum, it undergoes a kind of second digestion, by the movements of that organ, and by being intimately mixed up with the bile, pancreatic juice, and a juice secreted by the duodenum itself; by which process it is converted *into two substances*—one a white fluid, called *chyle*, and the other a yellow pulp, which finally becomes *excrement*.

The *bile* is a bitter, greenish fluid, secreted by a large gland, called *the liver*, which weighs about four pounds. It is from the *venous* blood passing through ramifications of the liver, that the bile is secreted, and, when secreted, is contained in the *gall-bladder* till wanted.

The *pancreatic juice* is a peculiar fluid, something in appearance like saliva, and is secreted from an oblong gland, called the *pancreas*, or sweetbread;—one end of it is attached to the duodenum, and the other to the spleen.

Whenever there is any chyme in the duodenum, both

these glands pour their juices into it, drop by drop, by means of two small pipes, or ducts.

When the food is thus converted into *chyle*, it passes into other portions of the intestines; first into the *jejunum*, and then into the *ilium*.

The *intestines* have three coatings, similar to the stomach, and, when active, the same worm-like motion. They have also, like it, their veins, arteries, nerves, and mucous ducts; and, in addition to these, are provided with a vast number of minute absorbent vessels, called *lacteals*.

These lacteals absorb the chyle in its progress through the before-named portions of the intestines, having their mouths, or openings, within the intestines, and being connected with vessels on their surface.

After its absorption by the *lacteals*, it is conveyed to the *mesenteric glands*, then into *the receptacle of the chyle*, then to the *lymphatic vessels*, and then into the *thoracic duct*, by which it is conveyed up through the body, and into the *jugular vein*.

The intestines are about four times the length of the body; a portion of them are disposed in folds, and attached to the spine by a membrane called the *mesentry;* different portions of them are distinguished by different names, such as the *duodenum*, the *jejunum*, the *ilium*, *corcum*, *colon*, and *rectum*.

THE BRAIN.

The brain is a soft, *medullary** substance, which completely fills the cavity of the skull, and is joined to the *spinal chord*, or marrow, which runs down the back bone.

From the forehead to the back of the head there is extended a thin, stiff membrane, in shape like a scythe, which separates the brain for a great depth into two equal parts, called the right and left *hemispheres* of the brain.

It is also partially divided into an upper and lower brain;—the upper part, which is by far the largest, is called the *cerebrum*, or proper brain; and the lower portion, the *cerebellum*, or little brain.

It is again divided into the front, back, and middle lobes of the brain; but those divisions are not so distinctly marked.

* Medullary—pertaining to marrow.

The surface of the brain is covered with a variety of winding cords, called *convolutions,* which vary in size and depth in different persons.

Adhering to and filling up the space between those convolutions, there is a membrane of a finer texture, filled with blood-vessels, called the *pia-mater;* and, between these, another very thin covering, called the *arachnoid* membrane.*

Proceeding from the bottom of the brain are various *nerves* of sensation and motion; some going to the organs of sense, and others to the skin and muscles of the head and face;—the nerves which supply the body and the extremities chiefly proceed from the spinal chord.

The brain is the seat of our *thoughts, feelings,* and *consciousness;* and any injury done to it, either by disease or a blow very soon affects the mental powers.

The *intellectual* powers are said to be situated in the front, the *moral* faculties in the middle, and the *animal* feelings in the back lobes of the brain;—and in proportion as they are properly exercised will they increase in bulk and power; but if not, they will shrink, and lose their efficiency.

In infancy the brain grows more rapidly than any other organ, but all its parts are not properly formed till about the age of seven years.

The brain of an infant weighs about ten ounces; of an adult, about three pounds and half; and, in some instances, when persons have studied very much, from four to four pounds and half;—the brain of Cuvier weighed four pounds thirteen ounces and half.

THE CIRCULATION OF THE BLOOD.

The blood is the great nourishing and sustaining principle of life;—as soon as it becomes impure, it generates disease; and as soon as it ceases to flow through the heart, life becomes extinct.

The whole mass of blood in an adult person is about twenty-eight pounds, which is forced, by means of the *heart,* through every portion of the body in about every two minutes and half; so that about seven hundred pounds of blood pass through the heart every hour.

The heart is a strong, elastic muscle, the inside of

---

* Arachnoid—like a spider's web.

which is divided into four compartments; the upper are called the right and left *auricles*, and the lower, the right and left *ventricles*.

The auricles and ventricles contract alternately four thousand times every hour, and at every contraction propel two ounces of blood through the different parts of the body.

The blood is circulated to and from every part of the body by means of *two distinct sets of blood vessels*, all connected with the heart;—the one set called *arteries*, because they convey the bright arterial or pure blood; and the other called *veins*, because they convey the venous or impure dark blood.

The great artery through which the *pure blood* is conveyed is called the *aorta*, and in its course from the heart it sends out different branches, like a tree; those branches send out still smaller ones, till at last they become so numerous and minute, that you cannot prick the body anywhere with a pin, but you will chance to puncture some of them.

This pure blood is continually nourishing the body and repairing the waste that is going on in different parts of it; and, what is surpassingly wonderful, the same material builds up and repairs muscle, bone, fat, tendon, brain, and every different substance of the human frame.

But in this circulating and repairing *it loses its healthly qualities*, changes its colour, and becomes dark, or what is called *venous blood;* and in order to purify it again, pure air is essential, and the *lungs* are the organs provided, in which it is purified by the action of the air.

And in order to convey it to the lungs, after it has performed its healthy purposes, the *veins* are provided, which are branched out all over the body, like the arteries.

When, therefore, the pure blood becomes venous, it enters *the extremest branches of the veins*, and from these into larger and larger branches, till at last it empties itself into two large veins, called the superior and inferior *vena cavas*, and by them is emptied into the heart.

From the heart it is forced into the lungs through the *pulmonary arteries;* when it is purified in the lungs, it goes back to the heart through four *pulmonary veins*, and then, by the contraction of the heart, is again forced by the great *aorta* to the different parts of the body; and so the circulation proceeds.

The particles of the blood are round and flat, and it is forced by the heart through the body with a force equal to about sixty pounds.

THE LUNGS.

The LUNGS are two light, spongy bodies, situated on each side of the *chest*, which, with the heart, completely fill it; they chiefly consist of small tubes, air cells, blood-vessels, nerves, and membranes.

The *windpipe* is the vessel that conveys the air to the lungs; but, previous to entering them, it separates into *two branches*, one branch entering the right lung, and the other the left.

These branches of the windpipe spread out, like a tree, into other branches throughout each lung, till at last they terminate in an innumerable number of small cells: the branches of the windpipe are called *bronchial tubes*, and the cells in which they terminate are called *air vesicles*.

These *air vesicles* of the lungs are so constructed that the blood shall be spread out to be purified over the greatest amount of surface; and unitedly they furnish a surface of *twenty thousand square inches*.

The venous or impure blood is forced into the lungs through the *pulmonary arteries*, and the purified blood is conveyed back to the heart through the *pulmonary veins*.*

The *pulmonary artery*, on leaving the heart, separates into two branches, one entering the right, and the other the left lung; each of these branches are spread out into in smaller and smaller branches, till at last they terminate in the *air vesicles* in a complete net-work of arteries.

The instant a person *inspires*, or draws the air into his lungs, the heart forces out a stream of venous blood (through the *pulmonary artery*) into the lungs to be purified; and the instant it meets the pure air, it is converted into pure blood by the chemical action of the air.

The next instant of *expiration*, or forcing the air out of the lungs, the blood so purified is conveyed back to the heart (through the *pulmonary veins*); but in coming, back

* These are named quite the reverse of other veins and arteries of the body, as the pulmonary *artery* conveys *venous* blood; but this anomaly is accounted for by their conveying blood *to and from the heart*, as the other arteries and veins do.

it runs first into the *minuest branches*, and these empty themselves into branches still larger, till it is finally emptied by the *large veins* into the heart.

A person breathes from fourteen to twenty times in a minute ; a man draws into his lungs at each inspiration from six to ten pints of air, and a woman from two to four pints.

The motions of *inspiration* and *expiration* are occasioned by the mechanism and action of the *thorax* (or chest), and the *diaphragm*, or membrane which separates the chest from the abdomen.

The air which is breathed out of the lungs *is vitiated and impure*, as it has imparted its *vital* properties to the blood, and brings out with it great impurities from the lungs ; hence the great evils occasioned to the constitution *from breathing in close and badly ventilated rooms*.

The lungs are also great *absorbents*, and will readily admit into the blood any noxious vapour or effluvia ; and hence the ill effects which often arise from breathing the fumes of turpentine, tobacco, and the flocoli and vapours of close factories and workshops.

RIGHTS.

Man, in a savage state, thinks it *right* to pursue his inclinations and indulge his propensities, *regardless of the welfare of others;* and all ignorant and immoral men think and act in much the same way as the savage.

But all cultivated and rational men perceive that such selfish and ignorant conduct produces continual violence and dissensions in society, and therefore they condemn it as *wrong*.

They find, by experience, that mutual forbearance, sympathy, and kindness, form the strongest bond of union between man and man ; and therefore they define *right* to be *reciprocal justice*, or *such conduct as shall best promote our happiness individually and collectively*.

Though they see this great moral principle of *right* daily violated among almost every class of men, *for want of proper intellectual and moral training*, they feel certain that, as men approach to civilization, will all their *laws* and *institutions* be based upon it.

The *rights* of individuals may be classed as PERSONAL, SOCIAL, and POLITICAL.

The PERSONAL RIGHTS of man are, *first*, his right to share equally in the common patrimony of heaven to all mankind—the earth, air, and the waters, from which all must derive their sustenance; *second*, his right to personal freedom, no man having a right to enslave him.

But though these rights clearly belong to every individual, upon *our* recognised principles of justice, *they can only be secured to him by the arrangements of society;* for in a state of nature, or in the absence of all law, one man's rightful possessions are violated to day, and become a stronger man's property to morrow.

The SOCIAL RIGHTS of man, or those which he derives from *society*, are, *first*, a right to have his personal or natural rights secured to him—*second*, a right to have the fruits of his intellectual or bodily labour protected—*third*, a right to have his person secured as much as possible against the attacks or violence of others—*fourth*, the right of private judgment in all matters of religion—*fifth*, a right to be properly educated, in order that he may understand and share in all the benefits of society.

But to secure to him these social rights, *laws* must necessarily be made and executed; and this leads to the establishment of a legislative and executive power, or a *political government.*

The POLITICAL RIGHTS of man are, *first*, a right as a member of society, of having his person and property secured, to determine, in conjunction with his fellow-men, how these laws shall be framed, and by what power they shall be carried into execution—*second*, to unite with them in investing the government they may appoint with full powers to enforce obedience to the laws, and to obtain from every man his just share of the national expenditure—*third*, a right to the freedom of speech, the liberty of the press, and of public meeting, so as to influence his brethren in favour of any measure *which he conceives to* be an improvement in the arrangements of society or the institutions of government.

DUTIES.

Every person who seeks to secure and enjoy his own *rights* is bound, on every principle of justice, to assist in securing and affording similar benefits to others;—*this constitutes his social and political duties.*

Every person, being immediately or remotely connected with and dependent on the whole human family, should

" do unto all men as he would wish them to do unto him ;"
—*this constitutes his moral duty.*

Independent of the reciprocal benefits to be obtained by the observance of these *duties*, nature has so wisely organized human beings, that, *when their moral faculties are properly educated*, they can enjoy no higher pleasures *than those to be derived from the proper discharge of their duties.*

A great number of distinct and specific duties are comprised under the two general heads referred to—the following are among the most important examples.

As a member of society, it is a man's *duty* conscientiously to obey the laws   the solemn expression of the public will for promoting peace, order, and security; and to revere all those appointed to administer and enforce them.

It is also every man's *duty* to labour bodily and mentally, according to his abilities; seeing that no *idle* man can be supported in society, but by throwing additional labour on others.

It is the *duty* of every father of a family to be frugal, temperate, and industrious, so as to be able to provide them with comfortable subsistence, and the means of proper education; and, by his prudent counsel and moral example, teach them to become useful members of society.

It is every man's *duty* to deal justly, act honestly, and speak truly, in every condition, state, or calling he may be placed in.

As every man's life and possessions depend on *wise laws* and *just government*, it is every man's *duty* to make himself acquainted with the social and political institutions of his country; and to make any sacrifice that may be necessary, in his endeavours to purify them from corruption, and to base them upon the principles of justice.

It is the *duty* of every man to embrace every possible means for *the acquisition of knowledge ;* and seeing that the want of proper education occasions so much social misery and political vice, it is his *duty* to assist in affording the means *of proper education to every member of the community.*

Ignorance and selfishness may lead men to neglect these several important *duties*, but they cannot long remain neglectful of them, *without suffering in some way the penalty of such neglect.*